AF889138

You Are What You RETWEET

140 Social Media Rules to Eat By

Jenny Westerkamp, RD

You Are What You Retweet:
140 Social Media Rules to Eat By
Jenny Westerkamp

Visit www.jennywesterkamp.com or e-mail
jenny@jennywesterkamp.com

ISBN-10: 098855920X
ISBN-13: 978-0-9885592-0-2

Printed in the United States of America

First Edition

Book Design by Randi Lesniewski
Photos by Grant Legan
Editing by Suzanne Fass

Image Attributes:
Approve by The Noun Project
Disapprove by The Noun Project
Silverware designed by Tobias Tuleby from The Noun Project
Bird designed by Thomas Le Bas from The Noun Project
Check Box designed by Nate Eul from The Noun Project
Television by The Noun Project

GRATITUDE

Feeling gratitude and not expressing it is like wrapping a present and not giving it.

—William Arthur Ward

I am filled with gratitude for all the people who have helped make this book a reality. First, thank you to my supportive family (Mom, Dad, Tim, Pat, Jim, Matt, and Jack), especially my dad for brainstorming the initial idea one April evening, my mom for encouragement to finish the darn thing, and my brothers for telling me straight up whether or not an idea was any good.

Thank you to Julie Burns for responding to my first e-mail titled "I Want Your Career and Life," and then for mentoring me the past five years on integrative nutrition and life in general.

Thank you to research interns Julia Casey, Emily Finnan, Mary Parsons, Chelsea Paulin, Christine Scarcello, and Sidonia Swarm for dedicating time to this project, under a tight deadline.

Thank you to my past and current clients. They are great teachers on what works and what does not when it comes to making solid nutrition a realistic and rewarding part of life. Also, a special thanks to client Brandon Bollig (@Bollig87) for his help with naming the book.

Thank you to Alex Cotie, RD, for reviewing my manuscript and providing additional insight and ideas regarding the content of the book.

Thank you to my flexible and patient editor, Suzanne Fass, for her fine work, especially during Hurricane Sandy.

Thank you to my close friend Randi Lesniewski (@colecreate), for her fabulously creative cover and interior design of the book.

Thank you to Grant Legan (grantlegan.com), for his skilled photography work with my professional headshot and website photos.

Thank you to Jennifer Boulos (@JenniferBoulos), for her expertise and assistance with the book's marketing and promotion plan.

Finally, a huge amount of gratitude goes out to all the wellness experts I learn from on a daily basis. While there are too many to list, just check out who I follow on Twitter!

THANK YOU!

DISCLAIMER

The information provided here is intended for general information only. It is not intended to be a replacement for professional medical diagnosis or treatment for a medical condition. Health information changes frequently as research constantly evolves. You should not rely on any information gathered here as a substitute for consultation with medical professionals.

This book consists of my nutrition and lifestyle recommendations, as well as commentary, to support wellness. In addition, I provide nutrition advice and counseling regarding lipid disorders that is not universally accepted in dietetics. This nutrition advice is not sponsored, endorsed, approved, or recommended by the United States Department of Agriculture (USDA), Food and Drug Administration (FDA), National Institutes of Health (NIH), or the Academy of Nutrition and Dietetics (AND).

STATUS UPDATE

STATUS UPDATE

Growing up as the daughter of an information technology professional, I was drawn to computers and the Internet at a very young age. I was using Microsoft Word at age five and browsing the Internet at eight. I created my own website at twelve, and continued to spend hours on the computer through my teen years. In 2008, during the fall of my freshman year at the University of Illinois at Urbana-Champaign (UIUC), Facebook arrived. Throughout college, I used Facebook as a personal tool and was "addicted"—something that most socially curious college kids can admit to at one time or another.

During my senior year at UIUC, I started a business with fellow dietetics student Katie Hamm and we created a website for future dietitians called All Access Internships. When some resistance from dietetics educators created an obstacle to marketing our great resource the old-fashioned way, I decided that social media marketing would be the solution to reaching our audience. Our combined eight years of experience on Facebook and our familiarity with the evolution of social media allowed us to capitalize on this Gen Y phenomenon for our new business. Five months before our website's launch, we had a Facebook group that numbered over 1,500 members and was even mentioned in the *Journal of the American Dietetic Association* as a popular social network for dietitians—still before our website even launched!

With the success of social media marketing for my own business, I began consulting with established dietitians before I was "officially" a dietitian myself. I was paid to help them set up social media platforms and give recommendations on the best ways for their businesses to capitalize on social media. I was also asked to write an e-book chapter on social media targeted at dietitians, which ended up being packaged on its own by the publisher as *Social Media and the RD*. I am addicted to social media and fully appreciate its value, both personally and professionally.

Now: on to nutrition. When I started studying dietetics in college, I was unsure of what I would do with my chosen career until I met Julie Burns. Julie is a sports nutritionist in Chicago and owner of SportFuel, Inc. (sportfuel.com) and Eat Like the Pros LLC (eatlikethepros.com). She has worked with the Chicago Blackhawks, Chicago Bears, Chicago Bulls, Chicago White Sox, and many other elite athletes around the world. When I stumbled upon SportFuel's website the summer before my senior year, I read Julie's biography and immediately knew this was the career and life I wanted. So, logically, I e-mailed Julie with the subject "I Want Your Career and Life," and went on to describe how professionally enamored I was of her accomplishments and how I hoped she would take me on as an intern. Well, she did. And I realized quickly that my passion in dietetics lay in sports nutrition and disease prevention.

Going through my dietetic internship at Massachusetts General Hospital, my prevention passion grew with each patient who walked through the dietitian's door. Questions constantly popped into my head. How do I PREVENT people from getting diseases so that they don't have to see this dietitian? How do I stop the downward slope that people slide on when they follow the standard American diet full of processed foods? Every patient I met during my internship year—whether suffering from obesity, type 2 diabetes, cardiovascular disease, or any other *preventable* chronic disease—was a source of inspiration for a career in prevention.

After my internship, I became a licensed registered dietitian, and Julie hired me as a sports nutritionist for SportFuel, where I continue to work today. I am the team nutritionist for the Rockford IceHogs, an affiliate team for the Chicago Blackhawks, and I also assist Julie with the Blackhawks team. Over the past four years, I have been able to work with both athletes and nonathletes alike. As the nutritionist for a wellness center and a Pilates studio, I counseled clients on weight loss, food allergies, digestive disorders, adrenal and thyroid dysfunction, and overall disease prevention. I speak to a variety of audiences including the NBA Development League, local sports teams, fitness groups, corporations, and various organizations in the community. I love every minute of it.

Granted, I came a long way on my nutrition journey, so I can appreciate the journey that you may take as well. When I was twelve years old, I wanted to be a food scientist and develop the next popular flavor of Doritos. I really loved the Food Guide Pyramid, too, and thought that eating a stack of saltines after school was a genius way to get my 6 to 11 servings of grains per day. Now I believe that if people followed the pyramid, they would look like one! The cherry on top of all of this (no pun intended) was that I worked at Dairy Queen throughout high school and even had the nerve to continue working there through college—as a nutrition major! Five summers of Blizzards and banana splits. See? I have come a long way, nutritionally speaking.

As I learned new information on nutrition, posting Facebook updates regarding my newfound knowledge always created a stir. Once, I posted a picture of mechanically separated chicken (a.k.a. "pink slime"), the main ingredient in chicken nuggets, and received many comments from friends, even off Facebook! It was then that I realized nutrition and social media are two very popular topics that play significant roles, independently, in our young lives. Why not create a book that combines the two?

Checking your newsfeed every day is as natural as eating dinner. In fact, you might be doing these two activities at the same time. The fun part is that the strategies it takes to succeed on social media are the same ones you can use when answering "What's for dinner?" The goal of *You Are What You Retweet* is to present 140 social media rules that can also be applied to eating right. I hope to "feed" you the information in a way you will "like"! I'll compare Twitter characters to calories, embarrassing Facebook posts to dietary toxins, viral YouTube videos to food fads, Foursquare check-ins to eating locally, and LinkedIn connections to quality supplements. Puns are sprinkled throughout the book, all intended! Seriously, though, now is the time to start taking responsibility for what you put in your body and on your social media profile. Luckily, I will help you make eating real, nutritious food as easy as liking a Facebook status. Remember, you are what you retweet. So retweet right.

TRENDING

#nutritionadvantage

Social media affects your everyday life, so you can either use it to your advantage or disadvantage. #nutritionadvantage

Social media affects you. It affects your thoughts, feelings, and actions, whether you realize it or not. Assuming you are using it every day, you have the power to allow it to impact your life either positively or negatively. Whether you use it to your advantage, say, to network with a potential employer and land a dream job, or to your disadvantage by posting inappropriate pictures seen by said employer before an interview, social media can change your life. How do you get the most out of social media? How can you use it to your advantage? When can it work against you? These are questions I will answer throughout the book.

Nutrition affects you. It affects not only your weight, but your skin, hair, nails, mood, energy, and attitude. Really, you should care about what is on your plate as much as what is on your newsfeed. If you use nutrition to your advantage, you gain the benefits of high energy, easy weight management, positive mood, and prevention of conditions that could lead to disease. You can also use nutrition to your disadvantage, by making poor food choices leading to weight gain, poor sleep, constipation, low mood, and low energy. Are you 25 but feel like you're 50? That's a problem. Nutrition can change your life and you have the power to take advantage of it every single day.

#listentoyourbody

Social media is more than talking. It is about listening, too. #listentoyourbody

Social media is changing the way you communicate, collaborate, and find information that is both interesting and relevant. It brings you together with others in an interactive space where you can give and receive content in a way that has never been possible before. It is a two-way street, as many forget, where sharing and receiving information both play equal roles. By not balancing your talking with listening, you will not experience the potential of social media.

Nutrition is also a two-way street. It is not just about what you are eating, but it is also listening to your body and the signs it is giving you about your food choices. Just about every body function relates back to how you eat. In today's world, it is easy to experience food overload, whether in restaurants, at the ball park, or with snack foods in your own home. Pay attention to how you feel after consuming foods and appreciate the signals your body is sharing with you, as they are very relevant to your health. Are you sluggish? Do you feel bloated? Is it getting harder to sleep at night? Making this connection will allow you to understand that what you eat is just as important as how your body responds to it. Balancing your attention between the two will open the doors to the potential of nutrition in your life.

#foodindustryinfluence

The social media landscape has evolved rapidly within the last decade with the addition of corporate influence. #foodindustryinfluence

Although social media still serves its original purpose as a personal leisure activity, it has become a primary strategic marketing tool for small businesses and large corporations alike. Listening to and understanding what buyers are openly saying on social media platforms, companies can enter into these environments and engage with current and potential customers. This new influence of businesses on social media has changed its landscape, though; it certainly threatens your privacy as you are often allowing companies access to private information. It also affects your social media experience with the flood of advertisements and marketing campaigns.

While you cannot change this situation very easily, and of course you still choose to use social media channels whether ad-free or not, it is best to be fully aware of corporate influence and always stay true to your own personal decisions and actions, rather than be persuaded in another direction that may not be in your best interest. Can the value of social media outweigh its corporate influence? It depends on how you choose to use it.

....

Our access to food has changed drastically in just a short time compared to how long we humans have been roaming the earth. Within the last century, we have seen a boom of industrial food production. For example, in 1911, Crisco (cottonseed oil, originally an industrial waste product) was marketed as a health food. In the 1970s, soy lecithin (another industrial waste product, this time from soybean oil) was introduced. Think about margarine, Cool Whip, Egg Beaters, Velveeta cheese, and Wonder bread! These are all quite new to us humans. Our diets have evolved, although our bodies have not.

The food industry's new processing technology allows food to be readily available and stable on the shelves, but is this in your best interest or the best interest of the company? The motivation for more shelf stable food products was actually so that food companies would not lose money by having their products spoil before they could be sold. A longer-selling period meant better sales and less profit lost due to spoilage.

Now we have an overload of processed, disease-promoting foods that are readily available. Is it too much of a "good" thing? While you cannot easily change the country's food supply, you should be aware of food industry's influence over your food choices. Weed out the junk and make your own decisions on what is the best food for you, not what will make the food company the most money. (See #promotedfoods in What's Eating YouTube.)

#genYproblems

Generation Y has been on the forefront of social media revolution, creating expectations for convenience and quick results. #genYproblems

Generation Y, otherwise known as Gen Y, groups anyone born between 1982 and 2005. I will assume that you, the reader, are like me a part of Gen Y. Deemed the "technological age," Gen Y is in the vanguard of all things Internet and social media. In fact, on average Gen Y spends over three hours a day online. Social media is an extension of our personal relationships and we are likely especially savvy at it. In addition, we might also see the importance of balancing work and life and we value convenience. Social media is now in our hands constantly; we can reply to friends within seconds, and do quick Google searches anywhere. But don't let these conveniences get the best of you in. Building a strong social media presence does actually take effort and the results are not immediate.

....

In the same way, we search for a way to balance the good food and drink with the bad food and drink, and look for the most efficient way to feed ourselves. First we wanted easy. Now we want effortless. "Lean Cuisine in my microwave? Yes, please." Once, we wanted quick results. Now we want immediate results. "I would like to know what restaurant people think is the best. Actually, I want Foursquare to just tell me where to go based on where I have been in the past." And this can lead to unrealistic expectations: "I would like to lose 20 pounds. I would like to accomplish this is in six, maybe seven, days." Gen Y's attitude toward nutrition may be a result of our active social media use. However, just as with social media, you will get out what you put in. A simple attitude adjustment on the actual effort and expected results is necessary to succeed in eating right.

#returnoninvestment

Ask yourself what you want your social media return on investment to be. #returnoninvestment

Two of the most important questions to ask yourself before you dive head first into social media are what type of role you want it to play in your life and what you want your return on investment to be. Sample "returns on investment" could include improved networking within your profession, solid brand management for your business, higher quality educational experiences, or creation of new opportunities that help you reach your goals. What do you have to put in to get the return you are looking for? These returns will not happen in one day or with one tweet. Social media takes time. The effort you put in is directly related to the return you receive.

....

What type of role do you want nutrition to play in your life and what do you want the return on investment to be? Think long term here, as in weeks and months, not days. Sample returns may include weight loss, gained energy, improved sex life, better sleep, more alertness and concentration. The list goes on. Remember, eating well takes time and effort. Because you may eat out much more, are on the go, and have fewer meals prepared at home, it is hard to stay on track. However, the more effort you can put into educating yourself and making consistent health-promoting decisions, the more you will benefit and the faster the results show up.

BREAKFAST, LUNCH & TWITTER

twitter @twitter

#qualityoverquantity

Twitter is designed to share a lot in a small amount of content, so quality counts more than character count. #qualityoverquantity

Twitter is a form of social media that uses text message–like updates with 140 characters or less. The term "microblogging" has often been associated with Twitter due to the fact that users must tweet in a very concise manner within the character limit. This restriction popularized URL shorteners that leave more space for a message while still publishing a link. Established in 2006, Twitter has grown exponentially in the past six years and reports more than 200 million users (including verified celebrity users), more than 200 million tweets per day, and 1.6 billion search queries daily. Twitter isn't just "text-messaging"; since becoming highly popularized in business, political, and news outlets, Twitter has become seen as a way to get up-to-the-minute news of what's going on in the world. Within the tweet madness, content is king. Each tweet needs to be concise and compelling.

When it comes to breakfast, lunch, and yes, Twitter, the requirement is quality over quantity. Choosing real foods and focusing on the nutritional value of your food, rather than simply the calories it provides, is the biggest message I can give you as you begin to take advantage of eating like a champion.

twitter @twitter

#caloriesmatter

A tweet is only allowed to be 140 characters or less. #caloriesmatter

The technical definition of a "character" can be very confusing and involves coding language, but I won't delve into it here. To simplify, I can tell you that I know what counts as a character—a letter, number, symbol, or space between these. Taken together, these keep your character count moving closer to 140, the maximum number of characters in a given tweet. You can try to tweet over 140 characters but it's actually impossible, and you won't get out what you want to say unless you spread it over multiple tweets. This is pretty awkward. Don't do this. In fact, by doing this, you are missing the beauty of Twitter. Work within the constraints of the length limit, because it is there for a reason.

....

The technical definition of a calorie is the amount of heat required to raise the temperature of one kilogram of water 1° Celsius. Why do you put all your thoughts into calories? Now that you know it has such a boring definition, you should reconsider glorifying calories. I guess when looking at a food label you don't necessarily think of a calorie's technical definition. Rather, you might know that a calorie is just a unit of energy with which we fuel our body.

Yes, calories are important for maintaining energy balance. Your body consumes calories and it burns calories. The net difference between the two will determine your energy balance. If you consistently consume more calories than you need, you will certainly start to lose control of your weight. If you are consistently within your calorie needs or even a little less, your weight will be easier to manage.

Let's get something straight right now: I believe this generic message of "eat less calories" has been pounded into our heads because it is easy to understand. But this is just the tip of the healthy-eating iceberg (lettuce! Ha!). The real focus is not the calories (quantity), it's the nutrient density (quality).

twitter @twitter

#nutrientdensity

Make each character count. #nutrientdensity

It is easy to understand that your tweets have a character limit. What no one tells you is that *how* you use those characters is what really defines your Twitter skills. Your tweets should offer unique value to your followers. You only have so many characters, so what do you really want to say? Make each character count!

....

While we have to pay attention to our caloric needs, I think eating right is so much more. Nutrient density is defined as the amount of nutrients per calorie in a given food. Thirty-five calories of carrots and 35 calories of Cheetos have a much different nutritional makeup yet provide the same number of calories. Which is more nutrient dense? The carrots, of course. When it comes to eating, make each calorie count, and focus on the quality of what you eat. What should you really be eating to nourish yourself?

Eating all your calories in the form of a Red Bull, donut, Wendy's Spicy Chicken and fries, and pizza may be within your calorie needs, but won't get you very far in terms of body composition and health. You need to focus on meals that have high nutrient density and provide a solid base of quality nutrients, whether they are deemed high or low calorie. I suggest consuming both high-calorie nutrient-dense foods (such as nuts, avocados) and low-calorie nutrient-dense foods (vegetables). I also suggest avoiding foods with low nutrient density, whether they are high calorie (fast food) or low calorie (diet snack packs). What's the lesson here? Nutrition is not determined by calories. Repeat. Nutrition is not determined by calories.

twitter @twitter

#ingredients

Content is king. #ingredients

What is the recipe of a GREAT tweet? First, think like your followers and try to appeal to them. Don't assume that since you like something, everyone likes it, though. Tweets that I personally find worth reading include 1) a random thought or insight about a topic I am interested in; 2) promotion of a product or service, since I am already interested in the brand as a follower; 3) shared useful, educational information; and 4) posed questions that I am likely to respond to.

If your content is compiled of complaints, retweets galore, sad attempts at maintaining a presence with fluffy tweets (good morning, Twitter!!), or ridiculous one-on-one conversations with your BFF, then I don't want anything to do with it. Ironically, the tweets I find most annoying are ones that share what the person is doing right at that moment. Even though the original prompt for a tweet was to answer the very question "What are you doing?" it is no longer useful unless your followers are friends and family who would care about this. Again, try to appeal to the masses with the content of your tweets and give the people what they want.

....

The content of your food is king. The front of the box should not entice you to buy the food and—surprisingly—the amount of calories, fat, protein, and carbohydrates should not, either. What you are really looking at is the ingredients list. What is this food MADE of? What is its content? If you can't recognize the ingredients, put it back. If it is more than five ingredients, it is probably too processed. Put it back. If it's hyping the addition or lack of a certain hot nutrient ("now fortified with calcium!" or "no added high fructose corn syrup!"), don't be tricked into thinking it is healthier. It could very well have other artificial ingredients. Put. It. Back. In choosing foods, select those with minimal ingredients. And among those ingredients, you should know how to pronounce them and recognize them. Ever read an ingredient label on a carton of eggs? It says "Ingredients: Eggs." Look at what your food is actually made of!

GUESS THIS FOOD

When I was getting all into my nutrition courses, and being taught that calories were really all that mattered, I started to dabble in "diet" products to manage my weight. Alcohol apparently packs on the pounds, as does putting ranch dressing on everything. Want to know what my two favorite "foods" were? I list their ingredients here.

Diet Food No. 1:

Ingredients: WATER, PROTEIN BLEND (WATER, NONFAT MILK, WHEY PROTEIN CONCENTRATE, SOY PROTEIN ISOLATE), SUGAR, MALTODEXTRIN, CONTAINS TWO PERCENT OR LESS OF POLYDEXTROSE, CANOLA OIL, COCOA PROCESSED WITH ALKALI, NATURAL AND ARTIFICIAL FLAVORS, MAGNESIUM PHOSPHATE, TRICALCIUM PHOSPHATE, GELLAN GUM, CELLULOSE GUM, SOY LECITHIN, MONO- AND DIGLYCERIDES, POTASSIUM CITRATE, ASCORBIC ACID (VITAMIN C), SALT, POTASSIUM PHOSPHATE, CARRAGEENAN, SUCRALOSE, CORN SYRUP SOLIDS, VITAMIN E ACETATE, VITAMIN K1, ACESULFAME POTASSIUM, NIACINAMIDE, VITAMIN D3, CALCIUM PANTOTHENATE, VITAMIN B12, ZINC SULFATE, VITAMIN A PALMITATE, FERRIC PYROPHOSPHATE, PYRIDOXINE HYDROCHLORIDE (VITAMIN B6), RIBOFLAVIN (VITAMIN B2), MANGANESE SULFATE, THIAMIN HYDROCHLORIDE (VITAMIN B1), POTASSIUM IODIDE, FOLIC ACID, BIOTIN, CHROMIUM CHLORIDE,

SODIUM MOLYBDATE, SODIUM SELENITE. SWEETENED WITH NUTRITIVE SWEETENERS AND NONNUTRITIVE SWEETENERS.

This is . . . a Special K Chocolate Protein Shake (Chemicals! Synthetic nutrients! Artificial sweeteners!)

Source: www.specialk.com/protein-shakes/chocolate/

Diet Food No. 2:

INGREDIENTS: WATER, VINEGAR, HIGH FRUCTOSE CORN SYRUP, CORN SYRUP, SALT, CONTAINS LESS THAN 2% OF PARMESAN CHEESE* (PART-SKIM MILK, CHEESE CULTURE, SALT, ENZYMES), GARLIC, ONION JUICE, WHEY, PHOSPHORIC ACID, XANTHAN GUM, POTASSIUM SORBATE AND CALCIUM DISODIUM EDTA AS PRESERVATIVES, YEAST EXTRACT, SPICE, RED BELL PEPPERS*, LEMON JUICE CONCENTRATE, GARLIC*, BUTTERMILK*, CARAMEL COLOR, SODIUM PHOSPHATE, ENZYMES, OLEORESIN PAPRIKA. *DRIED.

This is . . . Kraft Fat-Free Italian Dressing (This was chosen in an attempt to get off my ranch kick. However, I downgraded with the high fructose corn syrup, added sugar, and chemicals.)

Source:
www.kraftrecipes.com/products/productinfodisplay.aspx?siteid=1&product=2100064271

twitter @twitter

#lifestylechange

Twitter is a journey, and it begins with the first tweet. #lifestylechange

Many people sign up for Twitter and are unsure about how it works or what to do. While you may not have a full understanding of the effort it is going to take to become a successful tweeter, whether personally or professionally, know that it is a journey, and every Twitter journey begins with the first tweet. As you attempt to create a strong presence, engage with others, and even gain a following, you will learn along the way. Soon enough, the Twitterverse will be much less intimidating. Take the first step and learn as you go.

....

The initial uncertainty on Twitter relates to the initial uncertainty of a new way of eating. You may decide to change your diet and are unsure about how to proceed with this new lifestyle. For example, a New Year's resolution, a new goal for the month, a pledge to "eat healthy," sound like great plans, but the actual implementation and process can be more difficult. Just like learning how to navigate your Twitter account, it takes time to learn and master your diet changes. You will make mistakes along the way, no doubt. However, by listening to your body, adjusting your approach, and continuing to strive for better well-being, you will take what would likely be a temporary "diet" and create a lifestyle change . . . for LIFE!

twitter @twitter

#whyeat

Understand why you want to tweet, because this will influence what you share with your followers. #whyeat

Twitter began as an easy way to share short updates with your social circle. Since its inception, Twitter has evolved to serve many more purposes beyond letting your friends know that you are devouring a delicious meal at a trendy eatery.

Top 5 Reasons to Tweet

1. Enjoy its entertainment
2. Strengthen social relationships
3. Achieve professional gains
4. Educate yourself daily
5. Foster engagement between yourself and your followers

Everyone needs to eat to live, but many are living to eat. Understanding the healthful reasons for eating will allow you to make a stronger connection with your food and improve your overall relationship with it.

Top 5 Reasons to Eat

1. Enjoy food's flavor
2. Strengthen social relationships
3. Achieve health gains
4. Educate yourself daily
5. Foster engagement between your body and your food

twitter @twitter

#enjoyyourfood

Twitter offers plenty of enjoyment opportunities, so take a break from your hectic day and read a few funny tweets! #enjoyyourfood

Twitter is a form of entertainment, and there is something for everyone to enjoy. To start, follow parody accounts, memes, or your favorite celebrities or public figures. I recently followed WeirdHorse on Twitter, which chronicles the life of a very weird horse. Hilarious. Then there are movie quote accounts, like one that tweets daily *Dumb and Dumber* lines. Again, hilarious. With new parody accounts showing up daily, here are a few of the most popular ones to date:

> *Most Interesting Man*: From the Dos Equis commercials, the Most Interesting Man in the World makes a great meme of himself. Stay tweeting, my friends.
>
> *Condescending Wonka*: Join more than 800,000 followers as Mr. Wonka makes you question your own intelligence.
>
> *Scumbag Steve*: Scumbag Steve is modeled after an actual person, although his meme persona is probably the funnier of the two.
>
> *Awkward Penguin*: A penguin does awkward things and then tweets about it.
>
> *Bad Luck Brian*: A personal favorite of mine, Brian is always experiencing terrible and traumatic events that will make you laugh out loud and be thankful your life isn't this unlucky.

We don't have a sense of taste and smell for nothing, so savor the flavor of food. It is meant to be enjoyed! Should there be a food that I recommend you eat more of, if you don't like it, don't eat it. Know that it may not be love at first bite, though. Give it a shot, because you can always unfollow that food.

twitter @twitter

#eatsocially

Strengthen social relationships. Tweet with family, friends, significant others, or potentials (wink, wink), but don't overdo it. #eatsocially

The growing popularity and hype prove Twitter's social influence. Its creation stemmed from the need to make a simple platform where users could easily share with their circle of close friends, essentially to strengthen their social relationships. Twitter allows users to share and connect at any time, any place, and for any reason.

Social tweets are those that connect with one or a few other friends, but do not necessarily benefit all of your followers (similar for them to being on the outside of an inside joke). Social tweets are appropriate, but should not be overdone! Use the 80/20 rule, where 80% of the time you are tweeting useful information to a majority of your followers, and 20% of the time you are having a Twitter conversation with just a few fellow tweeters.

....

Food brings people together. Sharing a meal with your family or your closest friends has amazing benefits. Sitting down to family dinners at night or dining on amazing food with people you love is one of the great pleasures in life. It brings people together and a bond is formed as a result of the shared meal.

Unfortunately, you may find that in social situations it might be harder to stay on track with eating purposefully. Know that if there is a benefit to your social health, then it may be worth deciding against your physical health for this "one time." Depriving yourself of having a piece of birthday cake on your birthday, if in fact you wanted to have that, is just plain wrong. In a similar way, if enjoying a cocktail—or four—with your friends is improving your social health in a positive way even though it may not be the best thing for your poor liver, then it does serve a purpose in your life. While social eating experiences are a part of a good life, know that temptations are bound to happen and you can make the best of it.

Giving in to social temptations should not be a habit. I suggest (again) the 80/20 rule of being consistent with consuming nourishing foods 80% of the time and keeping "social" eating (that may not be nourishing from a physical health standpoint) to 20% of the time. What you may find is that when you are able to nourish your body most of the time, you are in more control during social situations and do not go overboard with poor food choices. To start making better social eating decisions, eat slowly, choose one to two "gotta have" items, eat before you go, bring a healthy dish, or don't linger by the food. Also, when dining out, if you are full before you finish your plate, put your napkin and utensils over your plate to let your mind know that you are done. When you can combine the pleasure of social events with the satisfaction of making smart eating choices, you win!

twitter @twitter

#healthgains

There will always be a personal approach on Twitter, but goals to make professional gains should be defined and worked on. #healthgains

When you use Twitter as a professional platform, you must tweet with more of a purpose than when you are socially tweeting. Balance your approach between answering questions, giving advice, sharing tips, and promoting yourself without being too "salesy." These types of professional tweets should be done consistently if you are looking to achieve your goals.

Didn't know you could take your career to the next level on Twitter? Here are a few ways to make professional gains.

> *Expanding your network:* In the Twitterverse, you can make connections with like-minded people. Comment on tweets and initiate conversation with possible employers and customers. The environment created by social networking is conducive to just that—networking.
>
> *Keeping up with the Joneses:* If you can stay active on Twitter, then keeping up with what everyone is doing, reading, and interested in will allow you to better connect with them. You will better understand their needs.
>
> For example, as team nutritionist to the Rockford IceHogs, by following the players on Twitter I am better able to understand their personalities, activities, and overall motivation as athletes. I may even catch what they are having for dinner, too! Understanding this allows me to better connect with them and present nutrition education so that they will actually implement what I teach them.

Branding: You can use Twitter to brand and market yourself to your followers. Many people can get to know you in a very simple way by following your tweets. You are highly accessible to them just by being active on Twitter. The key is making sure you are presenting yourself the right way.

Eating is social, but it should always be purposeful. At the end of the day, your purpose for eating is to stay alive and fuel your body. Expanding on that, though, there are specific physical gains you can achieve, including weight loss, better sleep, improved sports performance, increased energy, and prevention or management of medical issues like hypertension, diabetes, and cancer. You use nutrition to make these physical gains and improve the function of your body in one or many ways. Nobody is perfect, and there is always room for improvement. Identify the mind and body benefits you want to gain through your diet. Then evaluate your progress based on the dietary changes you make every month. This is a process that can be repeated over and over again as you continue to take your health and wellness to the next level.

twitter @twitter

#educationaleating

Educate yourself daily. Follow others you can continually learn from, and share information that you find of value. #educationaleating

To me, the most wonderful thing about Twitter is that I can learn from others and spread this knowledge to my followers. Every day, I learn new things on Twitter, often unexpectedly! My advice is to spend at least as much time listening and learning as you do broadcasting and educating, and keep an open mind always.

You can learn by following trusted sources, credible news accounts, and leaders in your field. For example, I follow many dietitians and nutritionists, simply because they offer informative nutrition-related tweets. Then, share information, ideas, opinions, links, and knowledge (not necessarily your own) that you think followers would be interested in. You will be amazed at how much more informed you feel after reading through your Twitter stream and also creating new tweets each day. Oh, that subway accident that delayed the morning commute? Yup, saw it on Twitter and took another route. Boom.

....

Exposing yourself to food and nutrition knowledge is very empowering. The more you know about food and how different foods make you feel, the more confident you will be. Often my first step in working with a client is educating them on the topic of nutrition, before any specific recommendations are made. If you don't understand why you should be eating a certain way, then you are less likely to make the changes, right?

Check out who I follow on Twitter (@JennyWesterkamp) for my daily dose of nutrition education, because I am constantly learning, too. Besides learning from others, you can also do things like share your newfound love for olives, pass on your favorite egg muffin recipe to friends, introduce someone to quinoa, and encourage healthy patterns in your family. What's the point in learning all this new nutrition information if you can't share it? Spread that real food love!

twitter @twitter

#foodengagement

Foster engagement with your followers. You may be afraid of this at first, but it is necessary to function on Twitter. #foodengagement

You know you are a solid tweeter when you can foster engagement from your followers, meaning you are eliciting interactions and mentions on a consistent basis. This is hard to do at first. It usually begins with you initiating the engagement with those you follow to get the ball rolling.

Types of Twitter Engagement

Replies: Support those whom you follow by responding to their tweets, especially if they are asking for an opinion or proposing a question to their followers. It shows you are open for discussion.

Retweets: Retweet their tweets to your followers. You can either quote the tweet and add a comment or retweet the entire tweet. Retweeting was one of the first rules of Twitter etiquette because it allows users to give credit to the original tweeter.

Mentions: If you want to communicate with another tweeter in the public Twitterverse, you can include the @ symbol and then their username in your tweet (e.g., @JennyWesterkamp). They will check their Twitter profile for any recent mentions, and your tweet will show up. They may respond to you by replying to you in their tweet or may decide to direct message you and make the conversation private.

Direct Message: You can reach out directly to a follower, assuming you are following each other, and have a conversation in private within Twitter. This is appropriate when further discussion deemed not beneficial to your other followers is needed.

These four ways of engagement are the same exact ones you are looking to be done to you. With more replies, retweets, mentions, and direct messages, you can rest assured that you are choosing the right things to tweet. That type of engagement in social media is what makes tweeting worth doing. Without this engagement, it seems like you are just talking to yourself, no one is listening, and no one cares. That is what they call anti-fun.

....

Instinctively, we know we must eat. Without food and water . . . we die! (womp, womp) The fact is that we need food to survive and also to thrive. The original purpose of eating, as a human being, is to provide your body with nutrients to function. When it comes down to it, your relationship with food should be one of engagement. Good-quality input (food) will result in your body's engagement in the form of positive signals and responses, such as real food cravings, hunger management, mental focus, and stable mood. Yesssssssss.

twitter @twitter

#defineyourdiet

Get a handle on your Twitter handle. #defineyourdiet

When you sign up for Twitter, you are to choose a "handle" (a username in Twitterspeak). You will want to choose one that relates as closely to your identity as possible. Whether it is your business name, your actual name, or a version of your name, it is good to have a handle as specific as possible. Being specific in choosing your name will allow followers to get a general idea of what you stand for, since this handle becomes your identity in the Twitterverse. Note that every Twitter handle is unique, so you cannot copy anyone else's handle and they cannot copy yours.

With nutrition, your way of eating defines you. What works for you may or may not work for someone else. Your diet needs are truly unique, so focus on the quality and types of food that work for you. I define my diet as being composed of real whole foods that are nourishing and agreeable to my body. What's yours?

twitter @twitter

#genes

After you decide on a handle, complete your profile, which details who you are in—you guessed it—140 characters. #genes

When you create your Twitter profile, you are only allowed 140 characters to describe yourself. Your biography contains details that describe you and only you. Since limited space is allowed to sum up your super awesome self, you should think long and hard about what it says. This is the "bullet in the gun," as your profile is what potential followers will see first. What really matters, though, is that you "pull the trigger" and start tweeting!

....

While your genetic code is unique to you, your genes do not completely control your health, whether you have a disease, are overweight, or develop other health conditions. Genes provide the code that your body uses to make proteins for every cell in your body. These proteins control how every cell in your body functions. Your genetic predispositions may be the "bullet in the gun," but your lifestyle is what will "pull the trigger" on either positive or negative health status because nutrients affect genes.

In how you eat, genes are regulated by nutrients or a lack thereof. For example, vitamin D regulates over 1,000 genes in your body. If you don't have enough vitamin D on board, these genes may not signal the correct proteins to be made, which can disrupt your cells and cause processes like metabolism and mental health to go awry. So you are what you eat, but what if what you eat changes who you are? In fact, it does. Nutritional genomics (nutrigenomics) is the field of study that researches the relationship between nutrition and genes. Nutrigenomics was actually the reason I switched my biology major over to nutrition. I was barely staying awake in my genetics lecture when the professor started to talk about nutrigenomics. This area of study is concerned with how specific components in foods that you eat interact on a cellular level with the expression of your own genes. Holy science lesson! All you really need to know is that you have full control over your health and well-being because you control what you eat. Don't use your genes as your excuse for not fitting into your jeans!

twitter @twitter

#lifestyle

Your profile remains the same from day to day. Over time, how you treat your account will determine how you present yourself. #lifestyle

While your profile and Twitter handle remain constant from day to day, what can change is how you express yourself on Twitter. Twitter founders themselves are surprised at how their users have used their accounts. Originally intended to be a tool to keep up with your inner social circle, all the walls came crashing down and the possibilities for sharing pieces of information are now just about limitless. In order to get the most out of Twitter, you must put in the right amount and kind of work and maintain your account. How you use your account on a daily basis is up to you, but know that it affects your self-expression to the Twitterverse.

....

While your genetic code stays pretty much the same throughout your life, what can change is the lifestyle you are maintaining. Living a healthy lifestyle is work, especially in the unhealthy world we all live in. This work certainly cannot be done by anyone else but you. Decide what type of effort you need to put in and the choices you need to make to ensure you are creating positive health results. I know one thing for sure: it is not easy, but it is most definitely worth it.

twitter @twitter

#essentialnutrients

Even though you can technically be on Twitter and not actually tweet, this is not advised. #essentialnutrients

Don't be THAT account that has zero tweets. Active tweeting is critical to getting the most out of Twitter. Sure, you can listen by reading others' tweets, but it is essential that you speak up, too. If you don't speak up, then you give yourself limited chances to receive all the benefits of Twitter that we just discussed, including enjoyment, social health improvement, professional gains, education, and engagement.

....

Essential nutrients are vital to our life. They are essential because our body needs them but cannot make them on their own. Therefore, we must take action and eat them. Essential nutrients include macronutrients (protein, fat, carbohydrates), micronutrients (vitamins and minerals), and water. Macronutrients provide calories or energy and are needed for growth and metabolism, among other body functions; these substances are needed in larger amounts than micronutrients. Micronutrients such as zinc and iodine are necessary for the healthy functioning of all your body's systems, from bone growth to brain function. Water is considered an essential nutrient because it is needed for the digestion of food; it makes up most of the blood plasma, helps body tissues absorb nutrients, and helps move waste material through the body.

Nutrition science continues to evolve and identify new compounds that are deemed essential to life. All of these essential nutrients are found in the food we "are supposed to be" eating!

twitter @twitter

#onedietdoesnotfitall

Twitter is very much an open forum for discussion and collaboration. #onedietdoesnotfitall

Considering that there are over 200 million tweets per day, according to Twitter, the Twitterverse can be quite overwhelming. To put this number in perspective, if the number of tweets per day were written in a book, it would be 10 million pages long. Add your own flavor, find out what works for you and how you can get the best response when contributing to discussion and collaboration. Copying the style of another Twitter user may not work for you and your account, but it is okay to be unique with your tweets!

Regardless of whether it is in the Twitterverse, your refrigerator, the farmers' market, or a restaurant, there is always something new to learn about or experience. Relating to your diet, don't be afraid to try new things, and be open to something that may be unconventional. Just like on Twitter, you are always able to learn from different people and different ideas. One way of eating does not suit all. Customization is necessary based on each individual's needs (i.e., medical status, goals, activity). Know that you are unique and what works for one person may not work for you.

twitter @twitter

#smartcarbs

Tweet something that will remain relevant for longer than five minutes. #smartcarbs

Yes, Usain Bolt just won an Olympic medal in the 100-meter dash, but if you tweet about it, your tweet becomes irrelevant faster than the race itself. While these exciting observations or moments in life are often the easiest to tweet, they may not lead to more interesting followers, engagements, or retweets. Tweet information that will remain relevant for longer than five minutes.

....

When choosing carbohydrate sources, avoid those that may provide quick but not sustainable energy. The topic of glycemic index and glycemic load comes into play here. The glycemic index is a scale from 0 to 100 that represents how quickly a food raises blood glucose (sugar) levels. High glycemic index carbohydrates are found in processed food products with enriched flour or sugar as a main ingredient. Glycemic load takes into account both a food's glycemic index and the amount of carbohydrate consumed. Consuming a high glycemic load, such as a meal high in carbohydrates and low in fat and protein, will cause a spike in blood glucose (see the "Crap Carbs" list in the Appendix for examples). Your body overcompensates with an insulin response that sends blood glucose levels too low—the "sugar crash." Crashing leads to lethargy, fat storage, and hunger, all of which majorly sabotage fat loss. Ever had a bowl of cereal in the morning and feel tired and hungry not long after? Yeah . . . that's that.

Real food low-glycemic carbohydrate sources are slow to be used and are not refined or high in simple sugars (see the "Smart Carbs" list). Your goal in making a smart carbohydrate choice is to choose low-glycemic foods so that your energy lasts and stays stable after the meal. The benefits of consuming low-glycemic carbohydrates include a lower spike in insulin response (increasing a metabolic shift to fat burn), more consistent energy levels, and more effective hunger regulation.

twitter @twitter

#crapcarbs

Avoid tweets are just plain crappy. #crapcarbs

Tweeting "good morning Twitterverse" or "good night tweeps!" is crappy. Stop wasting your and your followers' time with this nonsense. Also, I don't need to know if you love or hate Monday this week. Then there's the quotes. I go both ways on inspirational quotes, but really, something inspirational that comes from your own mind is so much better. Continuing on this crappy tweet rant: if every tweet is a link back to your blog, this defeats the purpose of the microblogging beauty of Twitter. People don't want to read long, boring blogs. That's why they are on Twitter. Cut the crap, people. You may imagine that we want to hear how great your significant other is, but we don't. Stick to useful, relevant information as much as possible.

....

Our food supply is FULL of crappy carbohydrates (see the "Crap Carbs" list in the Appendix). Why? They are cheap and versatile for food manufacturers. Double bonus for them. Double trouble for you. Refined carbohydrates, even refined whole grain products, serve no role in your diet. People are led to believe that "whole grains" are whole foods, but not when they are processed. Just because something is made from whole grains does not mean the grain is still whole. Whole-whole grains are what I recommend, and even then, if your digestion is troubled, whole-whole grains should be reduced or eliminated while your repair your digestion.

Real food unrefined sources of carbohydrates are the way to go. They have nutrients, they don't cause stress on the body, and they are not man-made. A sweet potato, for example, contains nutrients that help your body actually metabolize the carbohydrates. So wise, that Mother Nature! A slice of bread has these nutrients stripped out of it, and when the nutrients needed for metabolizing the food are not found in the food, your body must use its stores to get the job done, leading to faster nutrient deficiencies. So foolish, we humans! Real food carbohydrates (smart carbs!) are designed to ADD nutrients to your body and if that's not what a food doing, then that is simply crappy.

twitter @twitter

#pureproteins

Tweet information from credible sources and become a master in a specific topic. #pureproteins

There are a lot of Twitter users out there. How do you rise above as a credible tweeter? Take a look at the sources you are using for your tweets. Are they credible? Users are more likely to be influenced by someone who projects an image of expertise about a certain topic or industry, compared to someone who tweets on anything and everything. I must admit, I tend to trust anything that certain tweeters are saying because I believe their sources are almost always strong. So in order to be a trusted tweeter, be sure to stay consistently credible and use sources that you can feel confident in.

....

Not all proteins are equally credible, especially when it comes to animal protein. The saying "you are what they eat" means that the diet (and treatment and overall health) of the animal influences the quality of its protein. I recommend pure protein at every meal because it keeps you full, is the building block for all your cells, and helps maintain lean muscle mass. Plants such as nuts, seeds, and beans contain protein, but I encourage protein from animals as well, since these contain the complete profile of essential amino acids and are more bioavailable, which means that your body can use them more effectively and efficiently. This assumes, of course, that the source is high quality. (See the "Pure Proteins" list for high-quality protein sources.)

twitter @twitter

#pollutedproteins

Avoid tweets that are misleading or are for your financial gain and not the benefit of your users. #pollutedproteins

Sure, if you have thousands of followers, why not use this exposure to your advantage? Of course, in an effort to maintain your credibility, there are a few things you should not do. First, do not trick people into sales pages, bad content, or a poorly constructed website, whether with an original tweet or a retweet. Definitely do not push products, either. This reflects on your image and people will quickly unfollow if they feel like you are polluting their stream with tweets that will help you and not them. It decreases your credibility in a big way.

I'm going to give this to you straight: The industrialization of animal and seafood production is really about financial gain for their manufacturers and has led to a downward spiral in how animals or seafood are treated and consequently the quality of the food that comes from them. Conventional animal products are now laden with hormones and antibiotics, deworming medications, heavy metals, and even the MRSA superbug. And their nutrient profiles have changed as well—not for the better, mind you. Fish are currently being "farmed" instead of being fished out of the ocean! Most farmed fish are being fed corn, and last I checked, fish were not fans of corn. Additional processing such as adding nitrates to cured meats, ultrapasteurizing dairy products, and turning real cheese into individually wrapped single slices are heavily polluting the protein sources available to us. It is these polluted proteins that deserve no credibility in my mind! (See the "Polluted Proteins" list to see what protein sources to avoid.)

twitter @twitter

#healthyfats

Initiate conversation with the big guns in Twitter. Everyone's afraid to do it, but you shouldn't be! #healthyfats

Initiating the conversation with high-profile tweeters, like your favorite hockey player or musical idol, can be intimidating. Don't be scared! These tweets are positive, keep things interesting, and should not be avoided. While it's not the norm, Twitter does make this possible for a reason. High-profile tweeters want this engagement, so why not give it to them? Just try not to sound like a superfan, duh. The worst-case scenario is that nothing happens. The best-case scenario is that they engage back, and add to your Twitter power!

Of all the macronutrients I discuss with clients and friends, fats always spark a tremendous debate. For decades we've been led to believe that all fat is bad. But contrary to popular belief, the right fats can literally make or break your health. Choosing quality fats will help you control your appetite, stabilize your blood sugar, and burn body fat. Our society's fear of fat actually scares *me*! The media and food industry have led us to believe that low-fat and fat-free food products are the solution. Have they worked for us so far? No! Refined carbohydrates are added to these products to make them taste good, sans fat. Plus, look at the ingredient labels on these products. I'll pass. Don't be afraid of healthy fats—you need fat in the walls of every cell. It even improves your skin and hair.

It doesn't stop there! You need fat to efficiently absorb fat-soluble nutrients (vitamins A, D, E, and K) in the food you are eating. Steamed plain broccoli, plain baked potato with zero-calorie "butter" spray—how tasty is that? Maybe if you added organic butter to your broccoli and full-fat sour cream to your potato, you might eat more of these nutrient-dense foods! Finally, fat can keep you full much longer than a freaky fiber-fortified fat-free snack bar would!

All right, so you may be scared of raising your blood cholesterol by including animal fats such as egg yolks in your diet. Fret not! Nature doesn't mess up. Dietary cholesterol from high-quality real food has little effect on your blood cholesterol levels. Cholesterol is found in the outer membrane of your cells, protects your nerves, and is a building block of your sex hormones. You NEED it!

Here's a fun fat fact: Did you know that farmers are known to feed pigs skim milk to make them fat because they do not get fat on whole milk? Enough said. (See the "Healthy Fats" list to see what fats you should be eating.)

twitter @twitter

#damagingfats

There is no need to bad-mouth people, because the reputation you are really ruining is your own. #damagingfats

Somehow it became commonplace to spread rumors, slander, and libel people over social media. Freedom of speech, I suppose? I think it's rude. Obviously no one cares what I think, though, because everyone seems to be talking the T-rash and with no immediate repercussions, either. But it's simply not good practice. Protect your reputation and think before you tweet. That's what drafts are for!

Since the industrialization of our food supply, and the introduction of Crisco (an industrial waste product turned glorified cooking product), damaging fats have flooded supermarket shelves, and no one is making a big deal about this. These oils you see on product ingredient labels can come from corn, soybeans, and "vegetable" (actually, more soybeans), so they are "natural," right? Fat in its purest form is healthful, but damaging fats—typically with a high amount of omega-6s—cause brain inflammation, bad moods, and blood clots. Remember, processed vegetable oils are man-made and damaging due to the harsh heat, chemicals, and processing techniques used. Protect your overall health status by avoiding damaging fats. They are bad-mouthing your body. (See the "Damaging Fats" list.)

twitter @twitter

#hydration

It's all in the delivery. Keep tweets fluid and easy to read. #hydration

Twitter is a delivery system, and your tweet should enter the Twitter stream with ease. There's no excuse for bad grammar, sloppy writing, poorly worded tweets, and unnecessary shorthand. And I'll state the obvious: always use correct spelling and punctuation and know the difference between your and you're, and their, there, and they're. These 140 characters should also not be wasted on excessive slang, foul language, or abbreviation overkill! They need to flow nicely.

Water is key for delivering nutrients throughout the body and is needed for metabolism. When you are dehydrated, your body stops functioning as smoothly as when it is fully hydrated. Your body can temporarily have difficulty with cognitive functioning (thinking!), blood flow, and waste elimination (pooping!). To stay hydrated, a general recommendation is to divide your weight (in pounds) by two to get the number of ounces of fluids you need daily (not including training fluids). Add an additional 16 ounces if you are working out. Ideally, include a pinch of unrefined sea salt in your fluid intake for better utilization. Filtered water, tea, coffee, fruits, and vegetables all contribute to meeting fluid needs. Those fruits and vegetables are the original vitamin waters! You should avoid tap water as it contains chemicals very harmful to the thyroid, including excessive amounts of fluoride and chlorine. Yes, avoid fluoride in your toothpaste as well! You only need these elements in small amounts (See #traceminerals in Get LinkedIn My Belly.)

Who says hydration has to be boring? Health-boosting hydration options include green tea and bone broths. Green tea has been shown to increase antioxidant activity in the blood, improve fat metabolism, support the cardiovascular system, reduce the risk of cancer development, and lower inflammation, and it has antibacterial and antiviral action. Bone broths (heated up like tea) are a nourishing option for fluid intake, as well as a good source of calcium.

twitter @twitter

#emotionaleating

Sharing your feelings on Twitter is normal, but oversharing and using subliminal tweeting can lead to getting unfollowed. #emotionaleating

Don't overshare. Just don't do it. While it can be addicting and even feel satisfying, it will also lead to people unfollowing you. You have to know the difference between what should be texted, direct messaged, or said on the phone only to your mom versus what should be tweeted. New on the Twitter scene are subtweets. A subliminal tweet, or subtweet for short, is when your tweet refers to a particular person without stating their name or directly mentioning them. Often it will be hashtagged with a #subtweet. Sure, if you tweet these sad lyrics which so obviously depict the situation you were in with an ex-boyfriend, then yes, that might somehow make you feel better, but it does not make me feel better, and therefore, I will unfollow you. If you are sad or bored, please take it off Twitter, and call your mommy.

....

On the topic of emotional tweeting, emotional eating comes to mind. Does breaking up with said ex-boyfriend result in an ice cream deficiency? Not that I know of. Yet oftentimes food choices are determined by emotions. Emotional eating is the practice of consuming food, usually "comfort" or junk food, in response to feelings (e.g., sadness or boredom) instead of hunger. While it is true that certain foods, like the sugar in ice cream, can increase serotonin production, thus improving mood, the impending blood sugar crash after will return you to a poor mood quicker than you can say "Why did I ever date him?" Plus, a great deal of serotonin is made in your gut, so eating foods that stress out your digestion will cost you in the long run! Take care of your serotonin-producer and it will take care of you.

Because emotional eating can create a downward spiral this way, causing you to overeat (by eating both when you are hungry AND not hungry), you have to avoid poor food decisions. To combat emotional eating, have a hunger "reality check" by spending 10 minutes doing another activity, and if you're still hungry afterward, have a snack (see "Snacks" list in the Appendix). Tame your stress with yoga, breathing exercises, meditation, or time to yourself. Stop being bored! Get out there and find a hobby. Consider seeking medical help if you feel like you are unable to control your emotional eating.

If you are dealing with an occasional low mood, food does have the power to legitimately make you feel happier, and it can be done in a really healthy way, assuming you are only eating when you actually hungry. Some foods that will help increase serotonin release are bananas, dark chocolate, free-range turkey, and wild fish. Come on, get happy! (See "Happy Foods" list.)

twitter @twitter

#ediblemeansnothing

Just because you can type it doesn't mean you should tweet it. #ediblemeansnothing

There is no censor button on Twitter. You are capable of tweeting anything obscene, inappropriate, or untrue. That is, until followers block you, report you for spam, and thus get your Twitter account shut down. Until that happens, though, anything's fair game. Fortunately, most of us refrain from this inappropriate tweeting style. In case you forget, though, remember: just because you can type it doesn't mean you should tweet it.

....

Just like on Twitter where you can tweet "whatever," you can eat "whatever." You are the boss on what you eat. There is no censor on your diet when it comes to what you decide to eat. So am I saying you should eat whateva? No. Just because it is edible does not mean you should eat it.

There actually ARE bad foods out there, contrary to popular belief. They are bad simply because they are not good. These include those featured on the lists of crap carbs, polluted proteins, and damaging fats, as well as food-like items that have come into our food supply in the last hundred years. These foods may be considered "safe" (even if no long-term proof of their safety exists), but it does not mean they should be consumed. Some "favorites" include:

Nondairy creamer: I'm sorry, but if it is not dairy, then what is it?

Cheese product: If it says cheese product, it means there is not enough actual cheese in it to call it cheese. So again: if it's not cheese, what is it?

Fluff: Great name, but it should never be eaten.

And the list goes on . . .

twitter @twitter

#superfoods

Be creative by using shortening strategies to say a lot in a short amount of space. #superfoods

The Twitter founders chose 140 characters since a text message is 160 and they wanted to allot space for the username when tweets are sent from a mobile device. Most important, Twitter's founders believe constraints inspire creativity, and that they do. Using words that are easy to shorten or using URL shortener services, you can pack everything you want to say into your tweet.

Some Top Abbreviations	
RT	retweet
#FF	follow Friday
PRT	partial retweet
#TT	Trending Topics
DM	direct message
FB	Facebook
MT	modified tweet
TFTF	thanks for the follow
AFAIK	as far as I know
b/c, bcz, or cuz	because
EM	e-mail
fav/fave	favorite
FWD	forward
GN	good night
HTH	hope that helps
IMO	in my opinion
TY	thank you
TMI	too much information
LOL	laugh out loud
YT	YouTube

Just like on Twitter, there are shortcuts to increasing the nutritional content of your diet. These shortcuts are called superfoods, and you should be creative when trying to fit as many as possible into your meals and snacks. Superfoods are foods that contain a lot of nutrition per serving, packing a powerful punch without using up a lot of space. Superfoods range from fruits (especially berries) and vegetables (especially dark leafy greens) to animal proteins, nuts, and even fresh herbs! Salmon, blueberries, green tea, and dark chocolate are tasty examples of superfoods. The omega-3s found in salmon are known to reduce your chances of heart disease. Blueberries contain high levels of potassium and vitamin C and have anti-inflammatory qualities. Green tea has a high number of antioxidants. Dark chocolate is known to lower blood pressure and is packed with antioxidants. Nature never messes up. These foods are low in calories, but super high in nutrients, allowing them to be an easy addition to your diet, contributing more value to each calorie you are consuming. TY Superfoods! LOL!

twitter @twitter

#emptycalories

Don't waste tweets on nonsense and fluff. #emptycalories

No one likes to follow the person who tweets nonsense. Each tweet is an opportunity to improve your Twitter status, so don't waste it with "empty tweets." Tweet purposefully or your status will start to quickly decline.

....

As with nonsense tweets, don't waste your eating opportunities with "empty calories." Remember that nutrient density is the amount of nutrients per calorie in a given food (see #nutrientdensity). Sodas, french fries, processed cheeses, and damaging fats are a few examples of low-nutrient-dense foods that when part of your overall diet will cause your health status to quickly decline. In my opinion, the biggest contributor of "empty calories" is refined starches. Avoid refined starches (white breads, white rice, pasta, white flours) as these lack key minerals and raise insulin levels that promote fat storage and may make you crave them more.

twitter @twitter

#easytodigest

Usability is key when choosing what to tweet. #easytodigest

Tweet topics are limitless, but the more useful, the better. Again, it comes back to defining your target market and understanding what they want to read. Think about tweeting interesting bits of information or an exceptional article that others would enjoy reading. The trick here is to keep your useful tweets to 120 characters, so that they can be easily retweeted to include your username.

....

Not everyone is able to digest all types of food. For example, people who suffer from celiac disease or gluten sensitivities are unable to digest gluten well. Gluten can trigger an immune response in which your body attacks itself and creates damage in the digestive tract. This damage results in inflammation and decreases the body's ability to digest properly. It may also do damage in other organs and tissues such as the brain, pancreas, and thyroid, and may trigger autoimmune disorders.

Lactose intolerant individuals have difficulty digesting milk products because they have insufficient lactase, the enzyme that breaks down the sugar in dairy.

It is also stressful to digest common antinutrients such as lectins and phytates. Lectins are found in grains, nightshade vegetables (e.g. tomatoes, eggplant, bell peppers), soy, legumes, and nuts. Overconsumption may cause gastrointestinal distress by interacting with gut epithelial cells and causing damage. It may also cause leptin resistance, a precursor to obesity, cardiovascular disease, and diabetes. Phytates (found in grains, nuts, and seeds) decrease bioavailability of minerals. So, although whole-whole grains and real food like nuts and seeds have vitamins and minerals, some people may not be able to absorb them. But wait, there's hope! You can soak, sprout, or ferment these foods to decrease their lectin and phytate content, or buy already fermented foods and nuts and seeds that are already sprouted.

Choose foods that do not put added stress on your body and are easy to digest, and whose nutrients you can assimilate.

twitter @twitter

#timingiseverything

Tweet often, but not too often. Time your tweets strategically for optimal engagement. #timingiseverything

Do you ever get sick of those tweeters who are posting just about everything that comes to mind, with no filter? They are blowing up your feed, dude! Getting your timing right is important if you take tweeting seriously. While tweeting at least every day is recommended for the best experience, let's not overdo it. For multiple tweets per day, it is good to spread them out for a better chance that they will be read by different people throughout the day. And double bonus (love these)—you simply won't come off as annoying.

Opinion varies here, but posting content on Tuesday, Wednesday, and Thursday at 3:00 p.m. ET is optimal; this is when the most retweeting and commenting occurs, according to Twitter.

When eating, you want to eat every day, of course! But you don't want to graze all day or have all your calories in one sitting. After reading a lot of research on the benefits and pitfalls of consuming many small meals per day, my professional opinion is that you should be eating more satisfying meals so snacking or mini meals are not necessary. Often, clients are eating low-fat, high-carbohydrate meals (think salad with a couple ounces of lean chicken breast, veggies, croutons, and nonfat dressing) and are starving an hour later. Without healthy fats and more protein, a mini meal is often calling their name! If you change the meal to be more satiating, you don't need to eat so often.

With your meal timing, it is best to balance the quantity of your meals throughout the day. A quick rule is to take a look at your breakfast and dinner. Are they about the same in size? Often my clients who undereat during the day will be eating four to five times more calories at the end of the night than the total amount they ate during the day, which ends up surpassing their needs for the day. While there is no reliable evidence that eating late at night will make you fat, the problem is that people tend to overeat at night because they have not controlled their blood sugar well throughout the day and are now ravenous. Instead, eat relatively equal meals throughout the day.

In general, eating every four hours is a healthy schedule to strive for. As you change your diet and find foods that provide long-lasting energy, you will see that this is realistic timing. On the other hand, you do not want to go too long without a meal as this puts extra work on your adrenal glands, which are responsible for balancing your energy between meals. Your body needs fuel, and skipping a pit stop for food will cause more damage than good. Your adrenal glands will release cortisol (a stress hormone) to compensate for the lack of food coming in, and in the long term, excess cortisol output is linked to weight gain, especially around the midsection. Ruh roh.

twitter @twitter

#mealplanning

Schedule tweets ahead of time. #mealplanning

If your Twitter goal is to make an impression, gain quality followers, and engage, but you would also like to keep your day job, scheduling tweets ahead of time is a good way to still be connected and manage the daily task of sharing tweet-worthy information. Services available to get the job done include HootSuite, TweetDeck, and a Twitter mobile app.

HootSuite: This service allows you to manage all of your social networking sites (Twitter, Facebook, LinkedIn, Google+, Foursquare, MySpace, etc.) using one main application with one web address. This stops the hassle of logging into multiple websites to get your message out to your followers on all platforms. HootSuite will allow you to schedule when you would like to send a tweet, and then send that tweet without going to the Twitter website itself. You can also manage your favorite tweets, mentions, and direct messages. HootSuite also offers analysis of the engagement of your followers across multiple social networking sites. (hootsuite.com)

TweetDeck: This application is downloaded to a computer's desktop (Windows or Mac). It arranges your Twitter feed into customizable columns, schedules when a tweet will be sent to your followers, and gives you the ability to filter out tweets that aren't as important. TweetDeck can manage multiple Twitter accounts, for example personal and professional Twitter accounts. This application also notifies you when there are new tweets. (tweetdeck.com)

Twitter mobile app: This app allows you to access your Twitter feed and tweet from anywhere in the world, as long as you have your mobile phone and Internet access. You are no longer tied to a computer in order to tweet. You can also see trending topics and search tweets using this app. The Twitter mobile app is free for iPhone and Droid users.

....

What is the best way to feed yourself with nourishing foods without it feeling like it is a draining daily task? PLAN ahead! Schedule your tweets and schedule your eats, my friends. Scheduling meals will make the process less stressful. A common rule of thumb is that if you do something five times, it sticks. Plan your meals starting Monday through Friday. That's five days! See how you eat during those five days. You didn't go through a drive-thru or have takeout? Nice! Theme different nights of the week, too. Try spicing up your routine. For example, Taco Tuesday, Wild Card Wednesday (try a new recipe), or a—you know— leftovers night.

If you are ready to get planning, here are a few strategies for success.

Clean out your fridge and pantry: Search for recipes with items you already have on hand. If you have a lot of beans in your pantry, make chili. If you bought fish and it stares at you each time you open the freezer, it's time for fish tacos. This strategy will enable you to save money and discover new recipes with ingredients you already enjoy.

Keep your recipes organized and have an open mind: It is easy to get bored with the same recipe week after week. By keeping an open mind (stop judging the pot roast!), you'll never be bored. Also, by keeping your recipes organized and finding a good cookbook or website, you will have less stress and an easier time preparing your meals. There are a ton of free iPhone applications (e.g. Whole Foods

Market Recipes and The Food Lover's Kitchen) that make this a breeze.

Make it colorful: When visioning your meal, make sure there is a variety of color. (Ahem, nature's color. Mac and cheese is not nature's version of orange, just to be clear.) The more colors you add to your plate with fruits and vegetable, the more cell-protecting phytochemicals you will consume!

Happy planning!

twitter @twitter

#easytofind

Use hashtags so users can find your tweets, which could increase your numbers of followers and retweets. #easytofind

A hashtag is simply a way for people to search for tweets that have a common topic. For example, if you search for #glutenfree, you'll get a list of tweets related to the topic (assuming that the tweet contains the hashtagged phrase character for character). You will not get tweets that say "I love going gluten free" because the hashtag was not used here. Hashtags allow for both the creation and easy discovery of communities of people with similar interests. You can also get more followers and more retweets from people following a certain hashtag's activity. If you click on one of these hashtags, you can see who else has tweeted about the topic. A word of advice though: avoid using multiple hashtags in a single tweet. One or two is sufficient.

Using hashtags reminds me of making good food easy to access. For example, don't hide the vegetables away in the bottom drawer of your refrigerator. You'll forget about them! Put them on the top shelf where you can easily grab and devour them. Nom nom nom. Also, have healthy snacks in your drawer at work or in your car so that you aren't heading to the antinutrition drive-thru instead. Increase the accessibility of healthful foods, so they can more easily find their way into your belly. Get in my belly, healthy food!

twitter @twitter

#cautiousconvenience

While the convenience of Twitter can be a benefit, be sure to disconnect for a bit. #cautiousconvenience

Did you know that, according to the *Wall Street Journal*, 40% of all tweets come from mobile devices? In other words, nearly half of Twitter users are posting from the convenience of the mobile phone attached to their hands. With the Twitter mobile application and third-party applications like HootSuite and TweetDeck, tweeting can happen at the moment you wake up, when you go to bed, and any time in between. Don't take this convenience too far, though. Be sure to disconnect for at least a few hours during the day (if not more!) for your own sanity and the sanity of others around you.

Healthy eating needs to be convenient. #IGetIt. But don't let convenience get the best of you. Snack packs, bars, microwavable dinners, and shakes marketed as "health foods" are often some of the most disgusting and processed choices. Instead, choose real food snacks and invest in an insulated lunch bag if you have to. Seriously, it's not dorky. (Okay, well, I guess that depends on what it looks like.) But then you can have a hard-boiled egg on the go and not get sick from it sitting out at room temperature! Eggcellent! (See the "Snacks" list for easy—and easily portable—real food that's also really convenient.)

twitter @twitter

#keeplearning

Search for people, topics, buzz words to keep learning and stay updated. #keeplearning

By using the search function at search.twitter.com, you are able to look for people to follow and for informational tweets on a certain topic. Since the function is real-time, the page updates immediately as new tweets on your search term appear. Search for people, topics, buzzwords of interest. Study people who are credible, with the type of followers you want to attract. Model after their strategy. Use Twitter Search to see if people are talking about you, too! You never know. By entering your name, username, important keywords, competitors, or clients, you can find all the important conversations going on around your terms and follow the people having them.

Keep searching and keep learning about nutrition. See what others are eating, read cookbooks, do some research to see how you can improve your diet on your own. Sometimes it needs to come from outside inspiration. Watching the Food Network counts! Consider exploring nutrition blogs and websites, too. Some of my favorites include: Weston A. Price Foundation, Mark's Daily Apple, Balanced Bites, Underground Wellness, Charles Poliquin, Esther Blum, Jonny Bowden, and Timothy Ferriss. I am constantly adding to this list! If you need assistance in your learning journey, search for a nutritionist knowledgeable in real foods and wellness. They are the professionals and are trained to help.

twitter @twitter

#organic

Keep your tweets clean. #organic

No one wants to see you air your dirty laundry or see inappropriate statuses or pictures on Twitter. Keep it clean. Two celebrities with a large presence on the Twitter scene, Lady Gaga and Ashton Kutcher, disobeyed this simple rule. Lady Gaga tweeted: "Just killed back to back spin classes. Eating a salad dreaming of a cheeseburger #PopSingersDontEat #IWasBornThisWay." Followers found this tweet hypocritical since Lady Gaga usually promotes self-acceptance. Then Ashton Kutcher tweeted: "How do you fire Jo Pa? #insult #noclass as a hawkeye fan I find it in poor taste." This came after Joe Paterno was fired from Penn State for not dealing with his assistant's molestation charges. Gaga and Ashton got some serious backlash for these tweets. Yes, they are celebrities, and people hang on their every tweet, but you need to assume that people are looking at all your tweets, too. You want to project a respectable and clean image.

Like your tweets, keep your eats clean. If given the opportunity, opt for organic foods as much as possible. The application of pesticides on conventional produce is a concern because pesticides will promote inflammation, contribute to bone loss, and increase the risk of blood cell cancers such as leukemia and lymphoma. Some other agricultural chemicals mimic estrogen and can raise the risk of estrogen-related cancers. Dirty!

Organic foods are certified by the U.S. Department of Agriculture (USDA) in their method of growing, handling, and processing. In order to be "100% USDA Organic," the product must be made of only organic ingredients; to be "organic," the product must be at least 95% organic. The easiest way to identify if a product is 95 or 100% organic is to look for the organic green seal. What is known is that in organic growing, the use of pesticides and food additives are restricted. In addition, the environment is better protected, as organic farming practices are environmentally conscious. As an added bonus, organically grown crops generate phytochemicals (vitamins and phenolic compounds) for protection against insects, fungi, and other natural stresses of growing.

For produce, avoid the "Dirty Dozen," the most heavily sprayed produce listed below. For meat, poultry, eggs, and dairy, choosing organic means the animals were raised without the use of antibiotics or growth hormones. Choosing conventional animal products is a big "mis-steak."

A common myth is that if something says "natural" that it is organic. There is no exact definition of "natural" according to the U.S. Food and Drug Administration—and food corporations have abused this freedom when labeling as natural products foods with artificial dyes in them. Naturally, I am offended by this.

The Dirty Dozen

1. Apples
2. Celery
3. Red bell peppers
4. Peaches
5. Strawberries
6. Nectarines (imported)
7. Grapes
8. Spinach
9. Lettuce
10. Cucumber
11. Blueberries (domestic)
12. Potatoes

The following may contain pesticide residues of special concern:
Green beans
Kale/Greens
Source: Environmental Working Group

twitter @twitter

#favoritefoods

Organize your Twitter lists so it is easy to follow different categories of tweets. #favoritefoods

Lists, a newly integrated feature, allows you to create lists of tweeters in any category that you desire. Others can follow your lists and see the Twitter streams of those in that list. You can also follow other users' lists. Organization is the key to success, as my mom always tells me.

....

Just like you make lists of your favorite tweeters, make lists of your favorite foods in different groups. For example, you might list your favorite immune-boosting foods, your favorite protein sources, or your go-to real food snacks. You can't remember everything, you know. Keeping your list up to date with all your favorite real foods will allow you to stay organized and on track, without having to ask "what should I eat?" and struggling to answer your OWN question!

twitter @twitter

#beprivate

Use direct messages to take messages private and avoid annoying your followers. #beprivate

Direct messages are private messages, still 140 characters in length, that can be used for more personal conversation. In order to direct message a tweeter, you must both be following each other's accounts. This is so that there are no unsolicited direct messages. If you find someone interesting and are looking to connect in private, go ahead and let them know! That way, your followers don't need to be distracted by your one-on-one conversation.

....

Know that everyone is on their own journey, respect the privacy of other's food choices, and keep your own food choices to yourself, unless of course you are asked and are comfortable answering. On the same hand, there is no need to go on a rant explaining to people why you eat a certain way and why they should, too. If someone is paying you for your opinion, go right ahead (as in my case).

Often, when my clients are trialing a gluten-free diet, their friends may get very nosy about their personal eating decisions, and they are not sure how to deal with this. Eating is a private choice. Shame on people for trying to pry into others' choices for foods they eat. Imagine my life as a nutritionist. People judge what I eat and also think that I am judging them constantly. (Are you going to eat that cookie?)

If you do get asked about your food or food choices, and are caught off guard, you can simply say "I am working on a new wellness plan and still learning what works for me" or "I am working with a nutritionist. Here is her information if you want to learn more." I always tell my clients to blame me for their "unconventional" food choices. I can handle it!

twitter @twitter

#calorierestriction

Tweets do not have to be exactly 140 characters. In fact, tweets less than 120 characters are more likely to be read and retweeted. #calorierestriction

Just because you have 140 characters to work with does not mean you need to use them all. In fact, there can be an advantage to shorter tweets. Tweets less than 120 characters have been shown to be more likely to be read and retweeted. Less is more!

....

Calorie restriction is a dietary regimen that when applied properly and includes all essential nutrients may improve age-related health, slows the aging process, and promotes longevity in many animals and possibly humans. Research on energy-restricted diets over the years has proven that longevity is increased in many animals and fungi such as mice, monkeys, yeast, guinea pigs, rats, and some insects. There is also positive research to suggest its effectiveness in slowing the aging process in humans. In human subjects, calorie restriction has been shown to lower cholesterol, fasting glucose, and blood pressure. The research continues on the topic, but what I do know is that your caloric needs decrease with age, so healthy aging requires a reduction in the amount of food you eat to maintain your weight, assuming that other factors such as height, weight, and activity level stay the same.

twitter @twitter

#bethoughtful

Don't automatically send direct messages to new followers. #bethoughtful

Setting up an automated direct message to your followers may seem like a time saver, but it does nothing to build the relationship because the follower knows it's obviously not personal. Would you send a robot to network for you at a party? No. So let's not take the easy way out here. Be genuine, and put thought and intention into your direct communication with a new follower. Automating the process sends a clear message that your intentions were not for the benefit of getting to know that person.

....

Don't make eating an automatic process. Yes, you can get into a great routine with your new approach to food, but always attach thought or intention to all your food choices. Taking the easy way out with takeout is one example of lack of intention because it requires minimal thinking and it is convenient, but in most cases, you are getting low-quality food and not helping your body composition or overall health. Think before you eat!

twitter @twitter

#healthyinfluences

Look through your Twitter stream to decide who you really want to follow. #healthyinfluences

If you missed checking your streams for even a day, it's going to take you a while to catch up. You're busy—that's understandable—but if catching up with your Twitter stream is taking too much time, feels like an overwhelming flood of information, and isn't anything interesting or relatable to you, then edit your followers list. According to BrandSavant, 96% of Twitter users follow fewer than 500 people. Reevaluate your stream and get picky.

....

When it comes to nutrition, what is influencing you? Think about the quality of the food with which you surround yourself. If you need to, start over and look at food around you with a "fresh" perspective. Consider filtering and cleaning out your pantry. In the same way, what are the people around you eating? Are your coworkers or peers influencing your food choices negatively? If they drag you to the nearest fast-food joint, it's time to either ditch them or detour to a new restaurant. Just like keeping a healthy, useful stream on Twitter, do the same in real life by surrounding yourself with healthy options and influences.

twitter @twitter

#faddiets

Trending topics are appealing, but not sustainable or the key to gaining quality followers. #faddiets

Trending topics appear in the column on the left side of the page on the Home, Discover, and Search pages, and are determined by Twitter via an algorithm. They can be customized to any location. While trending topics are intriguing, there are new ones every day. It is not really a sustainable part of Twitter, and it's not meant to be, either. Beyond their here-today-gone-tomorrow nature, you can abuse trends in such a way that your account may be suspended. The following actions are considered trend abuse: 1) adding one or more topics/hashtags to an unrelated tweet or misleading link; 2) tweeting about every active trend, especially when mixed with advertising; 3) tweeting the same trend over and over again just to get the topic trending higher; and 4) combining trends with a request to be followed.

Fad diets are to nutrition as trend topics are to Twitter. While you may be curious what diet bandwagon everyone is jumping on these days, whatever it is is not typically sustainable or useful. In fact, it can be downright abusive to your health. You do not want to fall into the trap of a quick-fix mentality with fad diets. It did not take you a week to get to your state of health, so it will not take you a week to get out of it, either.

Let's be real. Who doesn't want to hear that you can lose weight by eating cookies and Twinkies? Actually, the answer to that hypothetical question would be: me. I don't want to hear about this insanity and you shouldn't, either. These diets, like many other short-term fixes, are based on the idea that no matter what, as long as you are consuming fewer calories than you are burning, you will lose weight. There are so many problems behind these diets. They are unsustainable and not contributing to long-term health. In fact, they can be considered self-abuse! Remember what we talked about in #lifestyle, forget about the here-today-gone-tomorrow fad diets, and focus on a sustainable way of eating for life.

twitter @twitter

#foodmarketing

Be wary of sponsored tweets and trends and the marketing bias behind them. #foodmarketing

Twitter has slowly been incorporating sponsored posts and tweets into the mix. Often sponsored tweets will have an "sp" at the end of them for disclosure and transparency purposes. Other random promoted tweets might show up in your feed, with a notification that it is promoted by a certain person or company. Advertising is not uncommon in social media, and with good reason. There is a market to be captured there. Obviously, the value you place on sponsored messages is your own personal choice; just understand that it is not as authentic as an unsponsored tweet on the same topic or company, where profit is not involved.

....

First, whether you know this or not, the information you hear in the media about nutrition is heavily influenced by big food companies. It is all about making money, so their goal is to make the cheapest food possible at the cost of nutrition. These long-touted convenience foods, snack packs, and low-calorie, low-fat highly processed products are not working for us. As a society, we still continue to suffer from obesity, autism, infertility, and for teens acne, food allergies, dental cavities all virtually nonexistent about a century ago before the onslaught of processed foods!

Sponsored diets promoted by the food industry are even worse. Remember the Taco Bell Drive-Thru Diet that boasted you could drop the pounds eating there? Or the Special K weight loss diet, where you could eat refined cereal and lose weight? The most notorious sponsored diet might be the Subway diet, which promoted Jared as their weight-loss success story for eating heavily processed deli meats with added nitrates on refined grain bread. #hahahah

twitter @twitter

#smokepointsafety

Never get too heated. It's in writing!
#smokepointsafety

You've seen them before: Twitter fights! Heated debates over sports, politics, religion, or the best bar in town. It is unwise to take these online conversations too far, as all your activity on Twitter should represent a calm and respectable you. Keeping your cool on a "public platform," assuming your profile is visible to the public, is always recommended to avoid being held responsible for those actions in the future.

....

Raise your hand if you cook with olive oil. Oh no! Put your hand down. Never heat olive oil or any liquid (unsaturated) oil to a high temperature. All vegetable oils are susceptible to heat damage, especially extra virgin olive oil because of its low smoke point. The smoke point is the temperature at which the fat or oil will produce smoke (start to burn) and when its nutrient quality and flavor start to degrade. Even if an oil has a high smoke point, using it for high-temperature cooking is still not recommended. You can still enjoy olive oil without heating it by using it as a salad dressing or drizzling it over already-cooked vegetables.

So what to cook with instead? You want to cook with a solid (saturated) fat because it is stable and more resistant to heat damage. While saturated fats have gotten a lot of hate, there is absolutely a healthy side to them that you might not hear too often. Saturated fats are needed to help cell membranes function properly; your heart and lungs cannot go without them; they put calcium in our bones, protect our liver, and support detoxification. I suggest cooking with organic butter or ghee (butter from either cows or goats, with all the water and solids cooked out) or coconut oil. With solids, you also want to find versions of these fats that have high smoke points. And if you do heat these up too high and see smoke, stop, throw it out, and start the cooking process over again!

twitter @twitter

#chemicals

Keep out the spam. #chemicals

No one likes spam on Twitter. Spam is annoying and potentially dangerous to your computer. Third-party bots can take over your account and send messages and tweets to your friends against your will. These unwarranted messages can include raunchy advertisements or links to inappropriate websites. Awwwwkward!

Tips to Protect Your Twitter Account from Spam

Don't autofollow back everyone using third-party services. You should know and trust all the people you follow.

Block suspected spam users from your account. Spam users can be spotted if they tweet meaningless tweets, have a ridiculous number of people they follow but a low number of followers, or have jumbled usernames that look autogenerated.

If you have been spammed, immediately change your password and delete any tweets or direct messages that were sent while your account was compromised.

Be wary of suspicious-looking tweets from people you know. Never open direct message links or questionable links, ever! If someone sends you a message that says "LOL this is a funny picture of you (link)" then it is probably neither funny nor a picture of you.

Just like dangerous spam to your Twitter account, there are chemicals that can get into your food supply that may be dangerous to your health. Polyvinyl chloride (PVC) and the notorious bisphenol A (BPA) are the two most prevalent chemicals we have to deal with, and are both most commonly found in reusable plastic water bottles.

PVC can increase flexibility, among other versatile characteristics. But PVC is dangerous because it leaks softening chemicals called phthalates. Phthalates are not only used to soften plastic, but are also among the oily substances used in cosmetics, perfumes, and many beauty products. Phthalates are conveniently labeled on common household products as "fragrance." That new car smell or brand-new shower curtain smell is the pungent odor of the release of phthalates into the air. Studies have found exposure to low levels of phthalates can cause infertility and lower sperm count.

BPA is the most widespread chemical used in the production of plastic food and drink packaging. It is used to create the epoxy linings of canned food and harder plastic containers and acts like the hormone estrogen in your body. What food processors don't tell you is that the chemical was created over 70 years ago as a drug intended to promote healthy pregnancies. Though it was never used as a drug, the food industry saw no problem adding this pregnancy drug to a wide range of products.

Low levels of BPA exposure have been linked to a wide range of adverse health effects, including abnormal development of reproductive organs, behavior problems in children, cardiovascular disease, and metabolic changes that result in altered insulin levels, which leads to diabetes. And its use for canned food is the number one reason why 90% of Americans have it in their bodies. Recent studies have linked BPA to breast and prostate cancers, enlargement of the prostate, early onset of puberty, hyperactivity in children, obesity, heart disease, and diabetes. Both PVC and BPA are now proven to be toxic, endocrine disrupting, hormone level changing, and disease causing.

Tips to Avoid Chemicals

Avoid using plastic containers. That includes using plastic water bottles and heating foods in plastic containers in the microwave. (Plastic with the numbers 2, 4, and 5 are the safest, however.) Use glass when possible.

Use stainless steel, cast iron, glass, or quality enamel when cooking. Cookware of aluminum or Teflon is reactive and leaches toxic components into foods via hot or acidic conditions.

Look for products in glass bottles or aseptic cartons (i.e., Tetra Paks) and avoid canned foods, even those labeled BPA-free, as contamination can still occur.

Read labels and seek out BPA-free and phthalate-free products.

twitter @twitter

#vitality

Retweets and mentions are a sign you are producing high-quality tweets. #vitality

Track your tweetability by the number of retweets and replies or mentions you receive; they are a sign you are producing high-quality tweets. If someone deemed your content retweetable or comment-worthy, it provides you with Twitter energy and excitement, fueling you to produce more high-quality tweets.

Real whole food is designed to support your energy and vitality as a human being, mainly by supporting your adrenal function (the organ that helps you deal with stress). Supporting stress handling is how many define "health." Tap into how you feel when you eat certain foods. If you feel energized and satisfied, in both the short term and the long term, it is a sign of vitality! If you are constantly craving a snooze button or a nap, it means your energy is not being supported and your diet can improve.

twitter @twitter

#weight

Gaining new followers is a sign of positive improvement, but they may not be all high-quality followers. #weight

Followers are those that choose to include your tweets in their Twitter stream. Your tweets will show up on their Twitter stream along with the tweets of everyone else they are following. Users can follow you without your permission, unless you want to restrict your tweets, although this is not advised if you are trying to market yourself. Your number of followers is impacted by what you tweet and your social media presence. Interestingly, you can also buy followers these days, so keep in mind, you are looking for high-quality followers, not fake or bought ones.

....

Your number of followers is similar to your body weight, which you are looking to keep within a normal range for your sex and height. You may think that single number on the scale is the only thing worth tracking, but that is not the case. While you may have been bombarded with "losing weight," you should really be concerned with the type of weight you carry, also known as your body composition.

twitter @twitter

#bodycomposition

Focus on the quality of your followers. #bodycomposition

There is no need to obsess over the number of Twitter followers you have. While a larger number of followers is better, it is the engagement of the followers you have, not the number, that matters. A majority of your followers should be active, engaging, and helpful in your rise to Twitter success. What you absolutely do not want are fake followers.

Celebrities and politicians are notorious for buying fake followers. What's a fake follower? It could be a bot or someone who created a Twitter account, followed some people and is no longer active. Hundreds of followers can be bought for around $1,000. To determine the quality of your followers, you can go to Fakers (fakers.statuspeople.com), which will analyze your followers and provide your percentages of fake, inactive, and good followers. Aim for a high percentage of good, active followers.

....

There are many ways to measure health, and weight alone is not a reliable one. For example, an increase in weight could be due to water retention, increase in muscle mass, or simply not going to the bathroom in a while! Just like your goal is high-quality followers, your goal is high-quality body composition. Ever heard of skinny fat? Skinny fat means that the person is at a normal weight, but has a higher-than-normal body fat percentage. This is the result of poor nutrition and food choices and does not mean they are healthy.

When you focus on the number on the scale, you don't get the best indication of your success. Rather, track your body composition. Your body is made up of two major components: body fat and your lean body mass (LBM). Your LBM consists of mostly muscles, organs, bones, tendons, ligaments, and water (every aspect of the body except for body fat).

Types of Body Composition Tracking

Bioelectrical impedance analysis: A low-voltage current is sent up one leg and down the other. Since fat is poorer conductor of electricity than lean tissue, measuring the resistance estimates body fat within ±3%, depending on hydration status.

Underwater weighing: The displacement of water is used to measure body fat. Since fat is less dense than muscle, a person with a higher percent of fat will weigh less than one with lower percent of fat. This is accurate up to ±1.5%.

Skin calipers: Uses a caliper (pinching) tool to measure the thickness of skinfolds at key locations, to determine an estimated body fat percentage. The accuracy of this measurement is determined by how skilled the person taking the measurement is.

Biosignature method: Developed by Charles Poliquin, this method takes skin fold measurements from 12 sites in the body and correlates their values to hormone status.

Body Fat Ranges		
Classification	**Women (% fat)**	**Men (% fat)**
Essential Fat	10–12%	2–4%
Athletes	14–20%	6–13%
Fitness	21–24%	14–17%
Acceptable	25–31%	18–25%
Obese	≥32%	≥25%

#summary #twitter

To tweet well, make characters count, write information-dense tweets, keep streams useful, and aim for a strong following. #summary #twitter

#summary #choosequality

To eat well, make calories count, choose nutrient-dense foods, keep your sources useful, and aim for strong body composition. #summary #choosequality

FB STUFF YOUR FACEBOOK

facebook @facebook

#healthyfoodrelationship

Sharing can be an effective way to improve self-esteem while maintaining relationships with friends and family. #healthyfoodrelationship

Created by Mark Zuckerberg in 2004 from his Harvard dorm room, Facebook today has more than 600 million users worldwide. It allows you to create a personal webpage detailing any and all aspects of your life: school, work, social endeavors, sports, activities, and more. You are able to post pictures, videos, and links to your profile, and write to other users via personal messages or direct public messages on their profile walls. Similar to previous friendship-based websites such as Friendster and Myspace, Facebook started as a way for collegians to keep in touch with one another at their respective schools. Originally only intended for college students, Facebook is open to the public; reports from April 2010 estimate that 41.6% of the U.S. population has a Facebook account. With its infiltration into your daily life, you can become slightly obsessed with it, share too much about yourself or know too much about your friends, and this can influence your life outside the Facebook "walls." However, sharing can be an effective way to improve self-esteem while maintaining contact with friends and family. Strive for a healthy relationship with Facebook.

Nutrition is also part of your daily life, and the relationship can be taken to extremes. Developing a healthy relationship with food will allow you to take advantage of its influence on your life without taking it to an unhealthy extreme.

Intuitive eating is a way of thinking that rejects dieting and in turn creates a healthy relationship between food, mind, and body. You will learn to respond to your inner body cues because you were born with all the wisdom you need for eating intuitively. This can be complicated for many people because there are so many dieting and food myths they have believed and followed all their lives. It's about rewiring how you think about food.

Three Ways to Have a Healthy Relationship with Food

1. Praise healthy choices. Go ahead; pat yourself on the back when you make a good choice. Stand a bit taller and be proud of yourself. You are doing great!

2. Don't nag yourself about unhealthy choices. Old habits can be hard to break—no need to feel discouraged. Instead just try to redirect yourself to a healthier substitute. Want something sweet? How about a piece of 85% cacao dark chocolate instead of a candy bar? Looking for something salty? How about a small portion of nuts or olives instead of potato chips? If you slip up, try to think of how you could avoid that slipup in the future. Don't feel guilty! Guilt never did anything to encourage a healthy relationship with food for anyone.

3. Never use food as a reward. That is not the best path to creating a healthy relationship with food. Next time you find yourself saying "it's okay, I deserve it" as you start to grab a candy bar, try finding a different sort of reward instead. How about you take a nap this afternoon, or go get a pedicure (guys, too!). Or even better—go for a walk or take a yoga class. You deserve to live a long life and have a healthy relationship with food.

facebook @facebook

#dietarystressors

Facebook is meant to be fun, not stressful. #dietarystressors

Does Facebook stress you out? Do you find yourself constantly competing with yourself and others to be better at life? Galaxy Research reported that over 63% of respondents to a survey they conducted felt that social media was a big contributor to their stress levels. Wait, isn't this supposed to be fun and entertaining? The respondents said they felt anxiety and pressure regarding their need to constantly check statuses, comment, and share their own content. Maybe you can relate to the times when you feel like the pressure is on to write a heavily liked or commented status. Stress less, my friends!

Stress is natural. Your body responds to stress the same way your ancestors' bodies would when being chased by a tiger. But now, with the world we live in, the tiger never stops chasing us! Many researchers believe that evolution has not caught up to this, so the accumulation of stress will affect your health, at any age. There are many sources of stress, but dietary sources are what I deal with most often. The good news is you have full control over how much stress you eat.

facebook @facebook

#sugar

Identify what triggers high amounts of negative stress on Facebook and get rid of it. #sugar

You know what really busts my chops? Engagement photos. Goodness gracious. So now I have to hide all engaged people from my newsfeed. Sorry I'm not sorry. Understand that the purpose of Facebook is not to stress you out, but to make life easier by keeping you up to date with your close friends and family and to provide positive entertainment and a mental break from an otherwise stressful day.

Identify stress triggers during your Facebook activity and work to reduce or eliminate them, whether that means defriending someone, logging on less, or even deactivating for a period of time. Perhaps, when I get engaged some day in the distant future, I will go back to those engagement photo albums in search of the least lame poses possible. Then it will not be so stressful!

....

What is the most stressful food for the body? Refined sugar! Refined sugar is bad for you and I know you know it. Now you just need to believe it. Our carboholic ways are catching up with us. Many Americans today find their sweet cravings to be somewhat uncontrollable. In fact, they might consider themselves addicted! However, they are simply listening to their bodies, and their bodies are SCREAMING for the quick energy that sugar can provide! Biochemistry overpowers willpower and you are left victim to the endless snacking and cravings . . . while never REALLY feeling satisfied.

The time is NOW to break the cycle and start on your path toward refined carbohydrate sobriety. Let's understand the science behind this. Carbohydrates are quickly absorbed by your system and make your blood sugar levels shoot up. When blood sugar goes up, insulin is released. Insulin is a prostorage hormone. It promotes storage of the sugar in the cells. It ALSO blocks fat from being burned. Essentially, you are locking fat in your cells when your insulin is high. Following the spike in blood sugar, there is a dramatic fall. This leads to false feelings of hunger shortly after—another craving. The rise and fall of blood sugar throughout the day will create feelings of hunger. Long term, this pattern can lead to obesity, cancer, heart disease, and premature aging!

On labels, you may see refined sugar as: brown sugar, cane syrup, high fructose corn syrup, fructose, dextrose, fruit juice concentrate, granulated white sugar, malt syrup, sucrose, and syrup. High refined sugar foods include: soft drinks, baked goods, and processed foods. Artificial sweeteners aren't much better (see #foodcovers in What's Eating YouTube).

How do you get out of your body's way and break the addiction?

> *Start by adding more protein and fat into your diet.* Go slowly, while your body adjusts to the changes. Choose grass-fed beef, pasture-raised chicken and eggs, real milk, butter, ghee, olive oil, or coconut oil.

> *Swap out refined food snacks with real food snacks.* For example, grab an organic apple and natural almond butter instead of packaged peanut butter–cracker sandwiches.

> *Plan your proteins.* Proteins like meat and dairy can be difficult to just whip up for dinner. Planning meals will make it easier to incorporate protein in your daily life.

> *Cook with healthful oils.* Or at least—start cooking! There might only be a handful of quick-service restaurants that provide real food to their customers and use the proper oils for cooking. At home, you'll know the hand that feeds you!

When you cut back on sugar, your taste buds will get used to it. I promise. If you continue your carboholic ways, you may soon lose control of your blood sugar, increase inflammation in your body, accelerate aging, and promote the development of chronic disease, because you're putting a huge stress on your body! Besides sugar, there are many other stressors related to how you eat, and managing these stressors is key to wellness.

facebook @facebook

#foodjournaling

Sharing on Facebook keeps you honest and accountable for many of your actions. #foodjournaling

There are many ways to share your life on Facebook, either with a status update, photo, or check-in. Of course, Facebook is not a sharing free-for-all. It does, however, make you mindful of your day-to-day life, because what you choose to share is out there for all to see. Are there things that you spend your time doing that are worth sharing to Facebook? Not everything should be shared, but if you find that there is nothing you do that you want to share with your friends on Facebook, then maybe it is time to reevaluate how you spend your free time.

Sharing what you eat can be healthy! In fact, there are benefits to food journaling. If you're on your path to weight loss or are looking to make healthier choices, then a food journal may be just what you need. Recording the foods you eat in a journal—online or on a phone app—can help you see clearly what and how much you're eating and drinking every day. It can help you recognize patterns or problems in your eating habits. It also creates accountability, especially if you're showing your journal to a dietitian, fitness trainer, or friend. Being conscious of what you eat and even just reviewing it yourself has huge benefits.

If weight loss is your goal, then simply recording your foods and drinks in a food journal can show you where those poor choices and extra calories are coming from and help you target areas for improvement. According to the *American Journal of Preventive Medicine*, those who kept food journals lost twice as much weight as those who kept no journal. Food journaling can be tedious, but there are several options to make it easier!

FitDay Mobile ($1.99): The FitDay mobile app is great for keeping track of your food intake on the go. There are loads of foods already on the system that you can choose from, with detailed nutrition information for each, such vitamin and mineral content (more important than calories, remember!), but there are custom food options, too, if your food isn't in the database.

Food Allergy Detective ($2.99): Not everyone wants to use a food diary app as an assistant to lose weight, which is where the Food Allergy Detective comes in. Food allergies and intolerances are on the increase; allergy tests can be expensive and can't cover all foods, so more and more doctors are recommending the use of a food diary to see what foods you could be allergic or sensitive to. This app is ridiculously easy to use; you just need to tap on what you've eaten, then later on tap if you've had any reaction. It can track symptoms even hours afterward—these can be anything from abdominal pain to headaches. You don't even need to put in what is in the foods you're eating, as the app recognizes what ingredients are present and logs them all. You then have access to a graph to track the severity of your reactions from mild to serious. The app analyzes all the information so you can more fully recognize any food sensitivity or allergies.

Calorie Counter & Diet Tracker by MyFitnessPal (free): This is seen by many as the ultimate in dieting and food journal apps. It certainly has the largest food database of any food diary app on the iPhone, with 750,000 entries. But there are custom options, too, and it even allows you store entire recipes and related information. You have access to all the nutritional information you need when you want to lose weight, including calories, fat, protein, carbs, sugar, and fiber. Another big advantage of this app is that it works offline, too, and you can back up your info to the website, so you needn't worry about losing any information.

facebook @facebook

#foodenvironment

Your Facebook friends affect the content of your newsfeed—and you are in control of who they are. #foodenvironment

When you log onto Facebook each day (each hour?), you view your newsfeed with great anticipation. Who's engaged, who broke up, who's hanging out with who and where. You must know. Going a step further, intellectually, what current events are people sharing that they find important? You likely find them important, too. Facebook friends' and liked business pages' updates are what make up the newsfeed's content, and in real time, too. In the ideal Facebook world, you should truly care about what's going on with these people and businesses, but is that really the case? Take control over your friends and likes and connect with those who make your newsfeed worth reading.

....

Your environment has an impact on your food behavior. Is it helping or hurting you? Take control of your access to food and your food options. This means that you identify the grocery stores with the best foods, restaurants with healthy options, and farmers' markets with the best produce. If there's a fast-food temptation that you drive by on your way home from work, can you take a different route? Can you bring your lunch instead of relying on low-quality cafeteria food in your building? Can you identify lunch spots that might be one or two blocks farther away, but offer organic chicken? Yes. Yes, you can.

facebook @facebook

#definingfood

Facebook has changed the definition of "friend." Bring back the value of real friendship. #definingfood

Before 2004, a "friend" was a person you actually spent time with, and there existed a valuable human bond between you and this person, sans the Internet (except for instant messaging, of course). After 2004, the definition of "friend" got a whole new meaning on Facebook. Now friend means that perhaps you shared one 15-minute conversation, or have a couple mutual acquaintances. Maybe you shared a class with this friend, but stopped talking to them immediately after that class wrapped up for the semester.

You still have to make friends in real life like we did pre-2004. That means you should not add just anyone you've ever come into social contact with. On that note, never add someone as a Facebook friend unless you meet them offline first! Don't let Facebook dilute the meaning of friends. Let's get real.

To bring back the value of friendship to Facebook, here are a few key strategies:

> Only write on a friend's wall, send a private message, comment on photos, or use chat *if you are actually friends with them offline*. Get the point?
>
> Communicate with your good friends using other methods besides Facebook. If you realize that all your interactions with a friend are on Facebook, it's time to work a little harder on that friendship or just let it go.
>
> Facebook can also reveal true—and false—offline friendships. Real friends don't post unflattering pictures of you, post statuses on your wall that could hurt your reputation or relationships or even your career. Pulling

shady moves on Facebook translates to pulling shady moves in real life. Are they really your friends? Nope.

....

Back in the day, people ate real food. A lot of what we define as "food" now would never have been considered as such a century ago. When deciding what is real food and what is fake food, ask yourself if your great-grandmother would recognize it if you put it on her plate. Would she know what a Twinkie was? Flaming Hot Cheetos? What about Kraft Singles cheese product? Go back to the original definition of food—a source of naturally occurring nourishment—not just anything technically edible that food companies say is totally great to eat in large amounts. If it is a new product within the last century that has been manipulated and goes against nature, then it is not REAL FOOD no matter what any commercial or advertisement tells you.

Value the true definition of food, and don't let it get diluted by food companies pushing their food-like substances. For example, they add milk protein solids to skim milk to make it look white (otherwise it is clear liquid), pump salt water into chickens to make them appear big and juicy, add dyes to cereal to make them look prettier, and add flavor enhancers like monosodium glutamate (MSG) to food products that without it would taste like cardboard! Are these foods really your body's friends? Nope.

facebook @facebook

#dietarytoxins

Toxins coming into your newsfeed are not helping you. #dietarytoxins

Sometimes easy access to your friends' lives is not a good thing. Take that ex-boyfriend and his posted pictures. Maybe you love that at least you know he has moved on, but these developments in his love life no longer affect you. When he keeps creeping into your newsfeed, it's time to detox. Take the girl who posts about her daily running, which includes the distance and time. Maybe you now know she is more fit than you, but it doesn't make you feel that good about yourself as you try to get serious with an exercise regimen!

Examples of Facebook Toxins

- Exes who may or may not be stalking you
- The chick who is always having a bad day
- ALL CAPS STATUS UPDATERS!
- The dude who hates Mondays—or any day really, except Friday, Saturday, or Sunday
- Old high school friends you wouldn't recognize if they didn't post a profile picture
- Runners who post their distance and time
- New parents who post 35 pictures of their baby . . . DAILY
- The girl with the new boyfriend, and they are obsessed with each other
- The person that posts a status both vague and depressing in order to elicit a "what's wrong?" comment
- The friend who just has to rant about politics, religion, or any other controversial topic

Toxins are energy sucks, giving your liver extra chores to do when all it really wants to do is hang out on its couch and watch the clean blood filter through as it should. Instead, it's been working overtime to keep you clean. Get rid of the toxins coming in.

Examples of Dietary Toxins

- Fast-food meals
- Artificial sweeteners (e.g., aspartame, sucralose)
- Overeating
- Damaging fats (trans fats, hydrogenated oils, myriad vegetable oils)
- Monosodium glutamate (MSG)
- Artificially colored and flavored foods
- Refined sugars (commonly found in processed foods)
- Conventional produce
- Cooking or reheating in plastic containers
- Alcohol

facebook @facebook

#diuretics

Identify your unworthy Facebook friends and defriend them immediately. #diuretics

Consider flushing out these Facebook toxins by having a defriend day! Even Jimmy Kimmel supports it, as he hosted a National Defriend Day on which he suggested you go through your friends and defriend any who are not worthy. Facebook friends you don't know well, don't WANT to know well, or are simply annoying are a time suck, and when you realize your time is being sucked it's time to cut the cord. Another defriending strategy is to look every day at whose birthday it is, and if you do not feel the need to tell them happy birthday, then you should defriend them. It seems like a big slap in the face to defriend someone on their birthday, but they'll never know! Just be sure you are not being irrational with your defriending. You wouldn't want to awkwardly refriend the person, because then they will definitely know you defriended them.

A diuretic is a substance that will promote urine production in the kidneys. Urine is one way we get rid of toxins in the body, so by encouraging additional urine output, you can help this process along. Make naturally diuretic foods part of your diet for a safe and effective way to flush out toxins. The most common foods that work as natural diuretics are beets, tomatoes, watermelon, cucumbers, watercress, and artichokes. Other foods that help promote waste removal in general are asparagus, Brussels sprouts, cabbage, carrots, and lettuce. It is important that natural diuretics are used with caution, as they can lead to potassium deficiency or dehydration if abused.

facebook @facebook

#detoxification

Take full advantage of Facebook newsfeed filtering to prevent toxins from building up. #detoxification

Sometimes you just can't avoid the toxins. Humans are unpredictable that way. Support the process of filtering your exposure to these people. You have that power, so use it! Here's how.

> *Sort:* Use the Sort menu in the top right of your newsfeed to choose which stories you see first. Click Most Recent to see stories in the order of posting, or click Top Stories to see the most interesting stories at the top of your newsfeed.
>
> *Browse lists and friends:* Click one of your lists on the left side of your home page to see stories just from the people on that list. To view posts from specific friends in one feed, find the Friends section in the left column of your home page and click on the name of the list.
>
> *Show in newsfeed:* Manage the updates you're subscribed to by hovering over the Friends button at the top of a friend's timeline and select Show in Newsfeed to turn their updates on or off.
>
> *Story types:* Select Settings to control how many and what kinds of stories you see from individual friends. Hide a person or a type of story (e.g., quizzes or games) by hovering over the top-right menu of a story, click the drop-down menu, and choose what you'd like to hide.

Our body has the natural ability to detoxify itself. This is done by the skin, liver, kidneys, and gallbladder, and happens in two phases. Phase I detoxification is the process by which toxic compounds are made water-soluble by the liver (essentially neutralizing the toxin). Phase II detoxification is when the neutralized toxin is released from the body as urine by the kidneys, sweat by the skin, or bile by the gallbladder. With the overconsumption of toxins in our food supply, especially if you are consuming alcohol or have a diet full of processed foods, detoxification support becomes a necessity so you can properly filter out these stressors on the body. (You also need to stop retoxifying!)

Diet Detoxifiers

- Organic produce
- Unrefined, cold-pressed organic oils in dark bottles
- Freshly ground flaxseed meal
- Green drinks
- Chlorella
- Filtered or spring water (8 to 10 glasses daily)
- Fresh dark green herbs like cilantro, parsley, and mint
- Undenatured whey protein from grass-fed cows
- Probiotics, prebiotics, and fermented foods
- Cooking with cast iron, ceramic, and glass (instead of Teflon)

There are many other ways to detoxify safely. For my best detoxification strategies, e-mail me at jenny@jennywesterkamp.com!

facebook @facebook

#seefooddiet

Don't be a "serial liker" and like every status you see. #seefooddiet

Like. Like. Double like. Love. Like. Like. Dislike. When scrolling through your newsfeed, if something stands out that you wholeheartedly support or agree with, go ahead and give that status a "like." However, if you feel the need to like every single status even remotely interesting, the person that wrote the status no longer values your like. Plus, it just comes off as annoying. Don't be a "serial liker."

Have you heard of the "see food diet"? If you see food, then you eat it. It's as simple as that. See that candy jar in the office? You don't even like vanilla Tootsie Rolls (who does?), so why did you just eat one? Just because you see it doesn't mean you need to eat it. Being picky is good, because when you make thoughtful food selections, you will find greater value in consuming them. You won't be desensitized to food because you won't be eating everything in sight. The "see food diet" takes the enjoyment out of food. Please. If you *really* like it, eat it.

facebook @facebook

#idealpoop

Positive notifications are a sign of healthy Facebook activity. #idealpoop

Notifications are alerts automatically created by Facebook that occur when people take action related to you. Examples of notifications include being tagged in a photo, invited to an event, or having a new timeline post. Notifications can be customized to fit your desires. They are available from your home page or from the notifications icon and can also be pushed to your mobile phone. Frequent, positive notifications are signs of an active and healthy Facebook experience. If your notifications start to diminish, or if they are not very important, consider changing your Facebook activity by posting on other's timelines, posting more of your statuses, and commenting or liking other statuses to improve notification activity.

....

What is my favorite health notification? POOPIES! That's right. Your poop, aka bowel movement, is a great sign of your overall health. You should be having one to three bowel movements a day. Beyond number, though, the size, shape, texture (ew), and smell (double ew) actually matter. Your ideal poop would be solid, medium brown in color, in the shape of a C or an S and pass "easily." Have you looked at (and smelled) your poop lately?

facebook @facebook

#notsoidealpoop

Then you have the not-so-ideal notifications. Those stink. #notsoidealpoop

Say you commented on a really popular person's status and now all your notifications are blowing up with stupid comments in the thread. Too much! Too much! Then perhaps you get in on a political debate (mistake!) and now you just aren't into it, but you can't help but keep reading. Time waster. Plus these notifications have nothing to do with what you really care about. Be aware of the type of not-so-ideal notifications you are producing.

Imagine talking with young male hockey players about their poop. Getting them to admit to not-so-ideal poop is probably the toughest part of my job, but it says so much about their health that I just must know.

When they do finally admit to it, they tend to have poop that is hard to pass and is thicker. I like to say it is "muscular" and they are okay with that because they think muscles are good. Oy. In this case, they are often overdoing it on processed meats and low-quality protein shakes and bars. I suggest real whole foods as much as possible, especially pure proteins.

What other notifications should you be looking for? Well, if you see pieces of undigested food, this could be low stomach acid or a food intolerance. Diarrhea could indicate a food that did not agree with you, in which case you should supplement with probiotics or probiotic-containing foods to bring your digestive tract back into balance. Poop in small balls is a sign of stress, dehydration, or lack of soluble fiber in your diet (which you can remedy by eating apples, oranges, strawberries, nuts, beans, cucumbers, celery, and carrots). Finally, if you're poop is super smelly, your diet stinks, too! It is likely too high in processed, conventional foods, and toxins, and possibly you overuse plastics in cooking and storage. Freshen up your diet so you don't waste all your money on air fresheners!

facebook @facebook

#immunityboosters

Build up your defense against unwanted visitors by using lists and adjusting privacy settings. #immunityboosters

Privacy is a serious matter on Facebook, as many Facebook naysayers say that we are underestimating how much private information the website really has on us. There are steps you can take to adjust your privacy, for your own safety. On a lighter note, take the example of my grandma's epic wall post: "Jenny you must check out Catholic Single website!!!!!! Love!!!" This, for all my friends to see. Love you, Grandma Wes!

First adjust your privacy settings. Limit sharing to your Facebook friends only, so you control who has access to your profile. Then turn off tag suggestions so facial recognition isn't used in photos of people you don't know. You might appear in a nonfriend's photo, but they will know who you are by Facebook's automated tag suggestions. It's creepy—and not safe. Finally, with the new timeline feature, I recommend that you limit the audience for past posts, so friends from 2012 can't see your posts from 2004. You've come a long way since then, maybe?

On to the lists feature, which are a more time-consuming but highly customizable privacy tool. This allows you to continue building your network without worrying about professional contacts seeing your personal updates.

> *Close Friends* will show up more in your newsfeed and you can get extra notifications of their activity.

> *Acquaintances* will rarely show up in your newsfeed, and there are no extra notifications available for them.

Restricted Friends are people you've added as a friend but just don't want to share with, like your boss. They will only see public content or posts you tag them in.

You can also create custom lists to organize friends as you prefer. Under Account, then Friends, create new lists, assign your friends to different lists, and customize your privacy settings accordingly.

It's time to take a closer look at how your immune system is protecting you from unwanted visitors. Your immune system's main role is to keep you from getting sick. Duh, you learned that in the fourth grade. What you might not know is that 60 to 80% of your immune system is your digestive tract. Making sure that your digestion is strong is key to keeping out invaders that could lead to sickness, food sensitivities, and autoimmune conditions.

You can boost your immune system with food, of course! Yogurt, kefir, and fermented foods like kombucha will boost immunity because of their probiotics. Probiotics are the good bacteria hanging out in your gastrointestinal tract that keep digestion (and therefore your immune system) in check. And garlic, which contains allicin, also fights infection from bad bacteria. Finally, listen to your great-grandparents who believed chicken soup was the best medicine. I am not recommending canned chicken noodle soup, but rather homemade chicken soup, especially the nourishing homemade bone broth!

facebook @facebook

#immunitydowners

Always err on the side of caution when sharing personal information; otherwise you put your safety at risk. #immunitydowners

Trust no one, not even Facebook friends. Always use caution when posting information about yourself. There are simply some things that you should never share, as they put your safety at risk. First, never reveal your exact location. While it's easy now to do this with the check-in feature on the Facebook mobile app, you can control whether this information is sent to all friends or just the ones in the list "Close Friends." Posting your exact location, especially telling people you left on vacation, may open the door for someone to rob you! You never know who is monitoring your activity. Second, oversharing personal information or posting a picture of your license or a private document could lead to identify theft. Keep this information off Facebook for your own security.

....

Stress, poor diet, alcohol, lack of sleep (perhaps from a poor diet), medication, inactivity, obesity, and dehydration are the most common ways to depress your immune system. Addressing your own immunity downers is the first step in protecting your health. Who *enjoys* having a cold for weeks on end? Not I. So get your immune system in check ASAP. It's for your protection.

facebook @facebook

#antioxidants

Do damage control on your profile. #antioxidants

On a regular basis, or at least before a big job interview, do some damage control and eat up any embarrassing wall posts or pictures, either by deleting them or making them visible only to you. (You can download your whole profile in case you are worried about losing the Facebook "memories.") This simple cleanup is a small but powerful way to stop Facebook from damaging your reputation, and it should be done often.

....

Oxidation, with the damaging by-product of free radicals, is natural process occurring constantly in your body. You need to balance this oxidation with ANTIoxidants in your diet. Antioxidants serve as damage control for your cells because they eat up all the free radicals in the body that can lead to chronic and degenerative diseases like cancer and heart disease. Look for foods with high ORAC values (oxygen radical absorbance capacity), meaning how well can they eat up the damage. The USDA recommends that we get between 3,000 and 5,000 ORAC units daily but on average, Americans only get around 1,200 ORAC units per day.

We do not need to find the next super fruit juice or supplement with high ORAC values because there are many foods at our grocery stores that in their natural form contain pack a high-ORAC punch. While I do recommend organic powdered green drinks for their convenient combination of high-ORAC ingredients, some whole foods to consume are cloves, ground cinnamon, dark chocolate, blueberries, plums, pomegranates, and goji berries.

facebook @facebook

#fasting

Sometimes it is good to step away from the 'book for a bit. #fasting

Ever feel like Facebook is becoming too much? If you are spending unhealthy amounts of time creeping around, giving up Facebook for the day or a week—or even just deactivating your account for a certain length of time—can be good for your soul. You could come back a more responsible Facebooker. Try it out and see how you feel.

The activity of fasting dates back to ancient times, when people fasted as part of religious and spiritual practices. Today, many believe fasting or intermittent fasting is a beneficial health practice. Short fasts may reduce oxidative stress and inflammation, and improve insulin sensitivity. And contrary to popular belief, short-term fasts will not mess with your metabolism. I often recommend experimenting with one-day-a-month fasts or intermittent fasting (see www.marksdailyapple.com and search for "Intermittent Fasting"). There are many different approaches to fasting, and certainly starting slow and under a healthcare professional's supervision is the way to go if you are interested in giving this a shot.

facebook @facebook

#cravingcontrol

Don't be a Facebook creep. Practice some self-control! #cravingcontrol

If there are one or two profiles you go to immediately and check more frequently than you eat, it's time to do some soul-searching. Are you a Facebook creep? A Facebook creep is someone who passes all of their free time on Facebook looking up details of someone they just met or may be infatuated with. They can tell you where that person is, and follow developments on the person's wall particularly closely (perhaps to spot competition). We've all creeped, but keep your self-control in check by keeping the creeping to a minimum. Your need to creep may be the result of something deeper than Facebook. Just saying.

Whether it's ice cream, chocolate, pickles, or chips, almost everyone gets cravings. So how do cravings work and why do we get them? Much of having a craving has to do with hunger, stress, or particular triggers.·The sensation of a craving is considered to be a sensation of "need" that we experience or as a "have to have it" feeling, arising from the midbrain area. The hormone dopamine is released when we eat foods we crave. Once dopamine is released it makes the body feel good, so obviously we want more of that food.

By giving in to a craving, you are likely not addressing the underlying cause of it—which is that something is missing. Instead of giving in to cravings, add boatloads of nutritious foods to your diet. Avoid processed sugars and excessive starchy foods that will promote high insulin production and cause insulin resistance leading to more cravings. Eat regular meals and snacks to control hunger, including balancing each meal with enough fat and protein, so what you eat does not cause a blood sugar crash and lead to cravings. Also avoid trigger foods and keep these foods out of your kitchen. If you don't buy 'em, you won't eat 'em. Finally, control your stress, as physical responses to stress include sugar cravings! Set yourself up for craving control.

facebook @facebook

#mindlesseating

While Mindless Facebook can be entertaining and enjoyable at the time, make sure you aren't doing this consistently. #mindlesseating

Facebook is an easy place to get distracted. You go to do one thing and then end up doing so much more and forgetting what your original purpose was. One time I got on Facebook to send an old college friend a quick message, but after reading other messages, looking at some photos, and changing my cover photo, I got up to get more coffee and completely forgot that the entire reason I got on Facebook was to send a quick message. This is called Mindless Facebooking. If you say this has never happened to you, then your pants are most certainly in flames right now.

Today two out of three Americans are overweight. Part of this problem is that Americans are not focused on how much they eat. The average person on an average day could make over 200 food decisions and not even realize it because they are distracted by something else. Whether the TV, the Internet (going on Facebook!), a newspaper, or a magazine, people often multitask while eating instead of taking their time to enjoy their food. This is called "mindless eating." To prevent mindless eating, separate food from technology by turning off the TV, computer, and phone. Eliminate all other distractions, as well. The worst thing is for the body to be under stress when eating, because this will impair digestion. Focus on your food and only your food!

facebook @facebook

#photoshoppingfood

Your profile picture should actually look like you in real life. #photoshoppingfood

Your profile picture should not be so Photoshopped and edited that it is no longer a true visual depiction of you. With great Photoshop power comes great responsibility. Plus, people will start to wonder what you are hiding behind those edits. Really, the most editing you should do in your profile picture is cropping out your best friends. They understand.

....

Fast-food restaurants are notorious for their false marketing and advertising campaigns that make their food look like perfection. Sure, it's smart marketing, but in reality, pictures on billboards, magazines, and commercials never match what you receive on your tray. Instead of crisp lettuce, fluffy buns, and thick hamburger patties, you received limp lettuce, dried-out buns, and dull burgers. What is hiding behind those edits? It doesn't stop there, either. Photoshopped food is just *one* type of misleading food marketing.

facebook @facebook

#fakefortification

Excessively editing your Facebook pictures will make others think you weren't satisfied with the original. Stay original. #fakefortification

Everyone knows that if the original had to be edited, it means that you looked worse than you do now. The integration of Instagram and its fancy filters makes photo editing more prevalent, although it is possible to be conservative with your edits and still look like you. When the edits are liberal, I question the originality of your pictures and how much they really depict who you are. Post positively and honestly here.

....

I question food companies that look to fortify and "edit" their food product. Shouldn't the original food we eat be good enough as it is? And if it's not, then shouldn't we be eating foods that naturally contain the nutrient they want to add in, rather than consuming an isolated and synthetic component? Fortification started because overprocessing stripped the nutrients out of the food. Although manufacturers make a lackluster effort at adding these nutrients back in with synthetic versions, it's like if you gave me $10 and I gave you back 23 cents. You just got ripped off. Think about that analogy the next time you are editing your pictures for a sepia glow (everyone looks better in sepia), while sipping a glass of calcium-fortified, DHA-enriched orange juice and eating protein-boosted fortified cereal. Eat some eggs and an actual orange, please!

facebook @facebook

#creepyingredients

Poking is for creeps and sends the wrong message. #creepyingredients

Don't poke anyone . . . ever. Back at the beginning of Facebook, poking was one of only a few ways to interact with a Facebook friend. Poke wars involved consistently poking back the user who just poked you. Who would give up first? Ah, those were simpler times. Now with the timeline, chat, messages, tagging, comments, and more to come, poking is on the bottom of the totem pole, rarely used except by people looking to either creep out a random or to elicit a laugh (and likely NOT a poke back).

....

Since food manufacturing of processed foods began ramping up in the late 1950s, there has been an astounding number of ridiculous additives sneaking into our food supply. While the Food and Drug Administration's term for these additives is "generally recognized as safe (GRAS)" they should be "generally recognized as creepy" and fall to the bottom of your diet totem pole.

> *Duck feathers* undergo heavy processing to become the primary source of L-cysteine, used in many fast-food bakery products.
>
> *Silicon dioxide*, also known as sand, is often added to processed beef and chicken to prevent clumping in fast-food chili.
>
> *Mechanically separated poultry*, commonly referred to as "pink slime," is a paste-like product created by forcing bones with attached edible tissue through a sieve or similar device under high pressure to separate the edible

tissue from the bones. It is found in a number of processed meat products like hot dogs, salami, bologna, burgers, and chicken nuggets.

Carminic acid is a commonly used red food coloring that comes from the dried, crushed bodies of a female scale insect called a cochineal. Beetle juice!

Tertiary butylhydroquinone (TBHQ) is made from compounds derived from petroleum and is used in a wide assortment processed food.

What are duck feathers, sand, slime, beetles, and petroleum doing in our FOOD?

facebook @facebook

#healthhalos

Don't believe every status. You never know what is going on in others' lives. #healthhalos

A friend might choose to post only positive things in her life, when in fact things may not be all fine and dandy. While this is your friend's decision, never assume you really "know" a person just because you are Facebook friends.

With the power of public relations, food companies can position their products to appear to be healthy so that the consumer buys them. Never assume that a product is healthy just because the company says it is. This perception of health-related qualities in one thing gives rise to the perception of similar qualities in related things. This is called a "health halo."

Terms such as "lower fat," "lower calorie," "natural," "multigrain," and "organic" are very attractive to health-conscious consumers' eyes. You might assume that this would mean the food was more nutritious. Don't believe every label or PR push. Yes, fruit snacks, you are "made from real fruit juice," but your flavor is strawberry and all I see is some apple concentrate!

My favorite health halo is "natural." The FDA and USDA have not come up with any real definition for the term "natural," so there are no restrictions. On a similar note, while the term "organic" is strictly regulated in its use, organic cookies are not healthful foods. They started with better ingredients, but the processing is still the same. Here are some examples of health halo food products.

Sports drinks: Sports drinks are meant for people playing sports, not watching sports! They are beneficial during activity longer than 90 minutes, and that is about it.

Otherwise they are a spectator's sugar water, and should be limited.

Heart-healthy margarine spreads: Margarine is not real food. It made from damaging fats, artificial colors, and artificial flavors, and is a product of the industrialization of food. Butter substitutes like margarine lack conjugated linoleic acid (CLA), which may be preventative of cancer, diabetes, and atherosclerosis. Eat butter, because when it comes to your health, there is no *margarine* for error!

Light salad dressing: The lack of fat on your salad decreases absorption of nutrients from vegetables and leads to greater spike in blood sugar. This dressing lacks cardiovascular benefits of healthy oils, and is usually higher in sugar and salt, with more highly processed ingredients. (Look again at the mysterious Diet Food No. 2 under #ingredients in Breakfast, Lunch & Twitter. Halo?)

Veggie burgers: Just because "veggie" is in the name doesn't mean a darn thing. Veggie burgers are often highly processed and their main ingredients are typically soy concentrate, wheat gluten, legumes, and various fillers and additives needed to achieve texture. Where's the veggie?

facebook @facebook

#fooddyes

Pictures might look good, but do they offer any value or do they just make you crazy? #fooddyes

Why did I just look through 176 pictures from my cousin's best friend's prom? Do I wish I were in high school again? Yes. Did looking at those pictures help make that wish a reality? No. They looked good, but it was a waste of time, and actually made me rekindle some negative feelings against the girl who beat me for Prom Queen. Rude.

The worst Facebook friends are the ones who post a ton of pictures, simply because you cannot help yourself from looking through entire albums for no good reason. You barely even know this person. You have not talked to her since sophomore year biology lab four years ago, so why can't you stop looking at pictures of her new apartment? Ugh.

....

Food dyes are frequently added to foods for purely aesthetic purposes: to add color to colorless foods, boost colors, recover color lost due to environmental factors, and to ensure consistency in variations of colors. Food manufacturers in the United States are allowed to use nine dyes approved by the FDA. Red 40, Yellow 5, and Yellow 6 are used in 90% of dyed foods. They offer no nutritional value and could be linked to health issues.

The Center for Science in the Public Interest (CSPI) pleaded to ban artificial dyes because of their connection to behavioral problems. The CSPI report *Food Dyes: A Rainbow of Risks* concludes that the nine artificial dyes approved in the United States likely are carcinogenic, cause hypersensitivity reactions and behavioral problems, or have been inadequately tested. Of note, Red 40 and Yellow 5 are undergoing extra scrutiny for being particularly harmful. Food dyes are found in packaged and processed foods, so eating more real whole foods instead will simultaneously reduce your food dye intake. Eat nature's colors instead!

facebook @facebook

#aphrodisiacs

Make your real life relationship Facebook Official. #aphrodisiacs

Facebook Official means a relationship with your significant other is now legit because you have changed your relationship status to "In a Relationship." Now everyone can see you are taken off da market. Feel free to change your status right in the middle of the day when most people will see it! You do have the option to not show any relationship status at all, or remove relationship changes from showing up on your newsfeed. This is if you want to keep things private and prevent brokenhearted embarrassment. Going Facebook Official can be a defining moment in your relationship! It can also be a deal breaker if your significant other does not confirm the request. If that's the case, he or she has some explaining to do, off Facebook chat, like in person.

....

Certain foods contain libido-lifting powers and can be used to improve your love life. Here's a fun fact: My go-to bachelorette party gift is now a cookbook full of aphrodisiac recipes. I won't say the name here, but it is always a hit! The secret behind love-boosting foods is the amino acid arginine, which is a precursor to nitric oxide that increases vasodilation (blood flow) to increase sensitivity and stimulation. Arginine sources include nuts such as almonds, cashews, walnuts, and peanuts. Watermelon contains citrulline, an amino acid that is metabolized to the stimulating arginine. In addition to arginine, other notable aphrodisiacs include: dragonfruit, chocolate, oysters, goji berries, truffles, avocado, figs, asparagus, and bananas. There are foods that can lower your libido, too, including a variety of processed grains, soy, mints (too much menthol), and quinine, the flavoring in tonic water. Better find a substitute for that gin and tonic, my friends!

facebook @facebook

#alcohol

Don't drink and Facebook. #alcohol

Alcohol and Facebook should never mix. Getting intoxicated and liking every status that shows up on your newsfeed is not what the cool kids do. Yes, you can Facebook in moderation while enjoying your party water (vodka), but overconsumption can lead to poor Facebook decisions. You are way too honest when intoxicated and there are way too many ways to share that honesty on the 'book.

....

As with drunk Facebooking, overconsumption of alcohol is never recommended, as it is a toxin and a stress on the body. Moderate amounts of alcohol do have benefits. Interestingly, one glass of red wine for women and two for men, per day, can support liver detoxification, while more can cause fatty liver, especially on those binge weekends. Beyond moderate consumption, alcohol interferes with the absorption and storage of vitamin B_{12}, folacin, and vitamin A. In fact, it may deplete the liver of its entire stores of vitamin A. What's worse is that because alcohol is a diuretic that increases the output of urine, it can cause the loss of water-soluble minerals such as zinc, magnesium, and potassium. To be honest, it's one of the worst things you can be doing to your body.

After a long night of drinking, do you ever promise yourself you will "never drink again" because of how hung over you feel? This could be a combination of dehydration, inflammation, hormonal changes, toxic load on your poor liver, and the OTHER impurities in the beverages besides the alcohol. And I am not even mentioning the poor food choices that could be made during or after a night of binge drinking, such as the burrito as big as your head.

Combat the hangover by simply drinking less, duh! If that doesn't work, mix in a water while consuming alcohol. Rehydrate with coconut water and electrolyte powder, liquid chlorophyll, or powdered greens. Consume liver-supporting foods like kale, Brussels sprouts, broccoli, and alfalfa, which contain glutathione compounds needed for detoxification. Finally, if you are trying to lose weight, alcohol is the anti–fat burner. First, it contains calories and should be included into your daily caloric allowance, but on top of that, it inhibits fat burning, making it harder to shed those extra pounds. If a friend is coming to me for advice on how to lose weight, I say to give up the alcohol for three months, and they will get great results, guaranteed!

facebook @facebook

#governmentisnotalwaysright

If Facebook suggests people you may know to be your friend, don't always take their word for it. #govermentisnotalwaysright

Facebook automatically sends you suggestions for people you may know using such factors as mutual friends, work, education, and networks you are a part of. While this may be helpful, there may be times when Facebook is wrong and you do not know this person, or you do know this person and would never dream of sending him a friend request! So take these suggestions with a grain of unrefined sea salt and choose your friend requests based on whom you actually know. Stick with making friends the normal way, through personal experiences.

Listening to everything that government organizations recommend on nutrition is a scary path to go down. The fact is that this information is more often than not tied to special interests from the industries that produce that food. It is a fact that our government heavily subsidizes the farming of sugar, wheat, corn, and soy, and these are the exact products they recommend should be a foundation of our diet. To make a joke of the situation, I often say that the MyPlate is like a billboard and whoever paid the most, got the most space on the billboard. Take these recommendations with a grain of unrefined sea salt, too, and read and study on your own for more unbiased information. A great read is *Food Politics* by Marion Nestle.

One of the most highly touted "health foods" of the past few years is soy. While fermented soy in the form of gluten-free soy sauce, miso, tempeh, and natto are acceptable, avoid processed soy such as soy protein isolate, as it contains phytates, enzyme inhibitors, and goitrogens that block the absorption of many minerals essential to our bodies (such as calcium, magnesium, zinc, molybdenum, manganese, and iron) and adversely affect the thyroid gland. Watch for soy protein in snack bars, too. Remember that the government subsidizes soy and soy is pushed incessantly. Most of the time, the form that the soy comes in is found in processed products, so it is no longer "real food." It is still processed, no matter how you look at it. This is just one of many examples of government recommendations I disagree with. Stick to eating foods that you know are real and work for you.

facebook @facebook

#gluten

Are you an oversharer? This is system overload! #gluten

No, you do not need to post 200 pictures of your child's birth. There is a time and place for everything, and sometimes Facebook is not the time or the place. You are overloading your friends' newsfeeds with this information, and it's creating undesired stress. Just because everyone is doing it does not mean you need to be a part of this ridiculous obsession to overshare.

You know what food component is seriously overloading our country's feed? Gluten! Gluten is a protein found in wheat, rye, and barley, with the most popular being wheat. Wheat is used in many food products today, but did you know grains are not a human requirement? Mind is officially blown.

Gluten is difficult to digest, and overconsumption of gluten has been linked to the development of food intolerances, digestive issues, fatigue, inflammation, and weight gain. Wheat centuries ago was not the same as it is now. There are fewer varieties of gluten-containing crops, plus the gluten content in these crops is significantly high. The content of gluten in wheat in the United States is the highest in the world. On top of that, our modern diets include many more gluten-containing foods than our ancestors ever ate. It truly is gluten overload! Take note that all the foods I listed in the Appendix are gluten free, so make an effort to at least go *gluten light,* as my hockey players like to call it!

facebook @facebook

#foodsensitivities

Sensitive topics used to be well avoided, but now there is a rise in their discussion and that can cause negative stress. #foodsensitivities

Sensitive topics such as politics and religion used to be taboo and were well avoided in "polite conversation." Now we are seeing a rise of these topics, especially on Facebook. I think it all started when Facebook allowed you to select your political and religious affiliations right on your profile. Of course, you have the option to omit this information, but many people are happy to share it.

While it is now becoming the norm to share political and religious articles on social media platforms, there are still real repercussions for doing so. Some users block, defriend, or hide those users' posts from their newsfeed because they so strongly disagree, or because they are just sick of seeing so many posts all the time. This rise in sensitive topics on Facebook can be a source of stress! Remember that not everything is "Facebook appropriate," so keep this in mind before posting.

Let's talk food allergies and sensitivities. First, to clarify, the terms "food allergy" and "food sensitivity" are often interchanged, but the conditions are actually quite different from each other. A food allergy is when the body has an adverse reaction to a protein in a food. The reaction occurs from immediately after consuming the food up to an hour later, and can range from mild itching to anaphylactic shock. In comparison, a food sensitivity is the result of the immune system's response to a certain food. The reaction may not occur until hours or days later, and may depend on the amount eaten. A common symptom of a food sensitivity is digestive problems.

To identify an allergy or sensitivity, one option is to go on an elimination diet and completely remove the suspect food from your diet for four to six weeks. Then reintroduce the food and keep a food diary to track the food eaten and the reaction that occurs when it is reintroduced. If you experience symptoms such as bloating, headaches, poor bowel movements, or fatigue, that food may not be the best for you right now and should continue to be eliminated to reduce stress and inflammation.

People with allergies and sensitivities almost always suffer from impaired digestion and a "leaky gut." This means that the food they've eaten has created such damage in the digestive tract that undigested food particles are leaking into their bloodstream. Their body does not recognize those particles and so attacks them as if they were invaders.

Avoiding foods that your body is sensitive to is a wise decision on your way toward wellness, since 60 to 80% of your immune system is in your digestive tract. While it seems like food sensitivities are taboo and you aren't being affected, they are on the rise due to the increased stress put on the digestion system by poor diet, toxins, and nutrient deficiencies. Don't make your body defriend you!

facebook @facebook

#signsofhealth

Look for signs that your timeline is portraying a steady amount of positive activity. #signsofhealth

The ideal Facebook timeline contains no spam posts, nothing embarrassing from family members, and nothing that could hurt you socially. It contains statuses with many "likes." Friends consistently post on your timeline. YAY! It is good to see positive reactions. It is not so good to see the opposite of these, or no reactions at all. If no one is responding to your wall posts to "Meet up later! Call me!" then something might not be right. Don't be oblivious if a relationship isn't working.

If you don't put the good stuff in, you become deficient. Keep uploading pictures, posting statuses, and liking or commenting on other statuses. Oh, and let's not forget working on these friendships offline, too. What you put in is what you will get out of it.

Every chronic disease is linked to at least one nutrient deficiency. Chronic disease is like having no wall posts in months, which eventually leads to people defriending you or totally forgetting that you exist in their social network. Look to your body's signals to determine if what you're putting in your body is contributing to your health or leading toward chronic issues.

There are many bodily issues that 20-somethings may think are normal, but simply are not. For women, PMS symptoms are not normal. For men, getting up in the middle of the night every night is not normal. For both sexes, neck or back pain, fatigue, digestive issues (e.g., constipation for more than two days), and inability to fall or stay asleep are not normal. Think about it this way. If you are taking something to help you eat right (diet pill), feel better (daily doses of NSAIDs), have energy (caffeine abuse), maintain clear skin (skin creams and treatments), poop (laxatives), or fall asleep (sleep aids, alcohol), please know right now that this is not healthful. These symptoms are signals that something in your body is not working and should be addressed immediately. See "Physical Signs of Nutrient Deficiencies" in the Appendix to find out what nutrients you could be missing.

#summary #facebook

On Facebook, filter your feed, handle unwanted stress, focus on real friendships, and pay attention to your notifications. #summary #facebook

#summary #lowerdietarystress

With your diet, filter your food, handle unwanted dietary stressors, focus on real food, and pay attention to your body. #summary #lowerdietarystress

WHAT'S EATING YOUTUBE

youtube @youtube

#somanychoices

YouTube offers so many choices, it is easy to be overwhelmed. #somanychoices

Sold to Google in 2006, YouTube was created by three former PayPal employees as a video sharing website. Viewers can watch music videos, TV and movie clips, and other uploaded videos. Registered YouTube users can upload amateur videos, and many even start video blogs that attract followers and a fan base.

While there have been concerns over copyright, piracy, privacy, and controversial videos, YouTube remains a social and cultural staple, with videos going "viral" and attracting millions of viewers worldwide. As recently as January 2012, YouTube reported that the site receives more than 4 billion views per day! Regarding viewing choices, 72 hours of video are uploaded to YouTube *every minute.* That's a lot of choices.

Entering a grocery store, you will see thousands of food products lining the shelves. As I started to study nutrition, without the realization of the food industry's influence, I frequented the grocery store not to purchase food, but to study what I then equated to "nutrition." HA! There is nothing nutritious about sugar-free, fat-free ice cream, but at the time, I thought that knowing about all these foods and recommending them would make me a better nutritionist.

When the party pounds began catching up with me, I decided I would give this whole "eat less and move more" concept a try on my own. I would run or work out six days a week and give in to all the low caloric treats, including low calorie Fudgesicles. What ended up becoming a Fake Food Free-For-All really served no purpose, as my energy crashed and I found myself digging into bowls of pasta for the first time in my entire life. I had serious carbohydrate cravings from lack of minerals (low "real food" diet) and impaired blood sugar management. There was very little fat in my diet, and my professors had taught me that protein can be a small side portion, so I barely had any of that. I was following all the advice that I was being taught in my nutrition courses, and was failing miserably. It was after my junior year of college that Julie Burns, my then mentor and current boss at SportFuel, enlightened me on what nutrition really is—and it is not in a protein-fortified cereal or bar.

While variety is appealing, the quality of these options can plummet with their increase in quantity. Our food supply contains the same kind of overwhelming number of options as YouTube, leaving us with little ability to get out of the grocery store in a reasonable amount of time. Instead, we linger in the aisles, comparing prices, deciding on flavors, choosing the lower-calorie option (so you can have more, right?), and throwing a few new industrialized creations into the cart.

Sorting through nutrition information these days can also be overwhelming! One minute a news report says we should eat more of a certain food and then a month later another report says the complete opposite. So how do you sort through the multitude of nutrition information and know what's REAL FOOD?

youtube @youtube

#highqualityfood

With so many videos flooding YouTube, look for indicators of high quality. #highqualityfood

There are several techniques to finding high-quality videos on YouTube. First, check how many "likes" (thumbs up) and "dislikes" (thumbs down) the video has received. This is one way viewers are able to gauge the video's appeal. Total views are good indicators as well, although just because they are popular does not mean they are worth watching. Check out the YouTube Charts page for a list of the top videos on YouTube where you can filter the chart by popularity, date range, and content category. These simple steps should lead to high-quality videos.

....

When shopping in a grocery store, you are flooded with new food products, sales, and marketing tactics telling you to buy certain foods. How can you know what food is high quality? First, shop around the perimeter of the store. This is typically where you will find fresh whole foods, as opposed to food found in packages that can sit on the shelf for a much longer time. Grocery stores need to easily swap out this fresh food before it rots or spoils, if it goes unsold. It is a good sign if your food is capable of rotting or spoiling!

Then avoid items that list wheat or enriched wheat as one of the top ingredients, as this usually means it is refined or processed and contains high amounts of gluten. Avoid products that have sugar or some type of sweetener in the top three ingredients as well. Finally, if you can pronounce and recognize all the ingredients on the ingredients label and there is no sign of any cartoons on the package, throw it in your cart!

youtube @youtube

#trustedbrands

Channels allow you to find more videos of similar quality and can be followed for easy viewing. #trustedbrands

Another way to find good videos on YouTube is to look for the people who published the videos you like. That means you have to click on the username of the person who uploaded the video; this will allow you to see a list of all the videos that they have published on their Channel. More than likely, they will have videos similar to the one you just watched. Surfing different Channels is a great way to find good videos on YouTube that you might not normally find.

Brands, like Channels, are an easy way to expand your food choices and discover new favorites. I develop brand loyalty to companies that produce high-quality products, and I am always willing to try whatever is new from them. A sampling of my favorite high-quality brands that are easy to find in grocery stores or online: Applegate, Organic Valley, Living Nutz, Living Intentions (Gone Nuts brand), Wellshire Farms, Earthbound Farm, Way Better Snacks, 365 Everyday Value Organic, Mary's Gone Crackers, U.S. Wellness Meats, Tera's Whey, Kerrygold, So Delicious (coconut line), Siggi's, and Kalona Super Natural. (Note: I have no financial relationship with any of these companies.)

youtube @youtube

#experiment

Simply spending time on YouTube and browsing videos will allow you to find what's right for you through trial and error. #experiment

One of the best things that you could do when searching for videos is to spend some extra time—assuming you have it—and just watch a bunch of videos! When you watch a video on YouTube, you will see previews of other videos that are related in one way or another to the one you watch. Trial and error allows you to get a feel for the types of videos out there. Even after viewing the video, you can browse the comments and feedback to feel more comfortable maneuvering through the bounty of choices.

....

When I go into Whole Foods Market or Trader Joe's, I am bound to pick up a few new products I have never tried. I suggest the same with my clients and you. Trial and error with foods is necessary. Buy it, and if you don't like it don't get it again. Sometimes the best discoveries were just taken as a chance. I recall my decision to go for the almond butter instead of peanut butter one day, and I have never gone back to peanut butter since. Adding new foods into your diet will be a process, but spending the extra time will allow you to discover some really delicious additions. Remember especially to notice how your body reacts to natural foods versus processed foods, too. We both know which side it will favor!

youtube @youtube

#cookathome

Create your own videos and upload them for the world to see! #cookathome

The ability to upload and share videos is what makes YouTube a force to be reckoned with. Now everyone can be a star! Videos do not have to be professionally done. They can be simple, which is what makes them so authentic and REAL. Directions on how to upload your videos are very simple. You can record directly from your webcam or mobile device. For the best results, use the best camera and best resolution you can. Be sure to use enough lighting to show the subject of your video. Finally, when uploading, add tags to help people find your video, and title it appropriately!

....

We have gotten away from the kitchen, many of us lacking basic culinary skills, like how to chop an onion. Really, the further you get from the kitchen, the worse off you will be. It is much better to cook at home so that you can control the ingredients, use unprocessed foods, and enjoy the act of connecting with your food. Know the hand that feeds you!

If you are on a full-fledged take-out diet, aim for at least three meals per week that you cook at home and eat in a low-stress environment (not in front of your computer or in the car). If you are cooking for one or two, preparing large portions of food to use over multiple meals saves time and energy. You don't have to be a trained professional chef to produce satisfying and simple real food meals. Everyone can be a cook, and we all should be!

youtube @youtube

#healthclaims

You can't always judge a video by its title or preview screen shot. #healthclaims

Have you ever seen a video with a title or preview screen shot that does not actually describe what the video is about? While we automatically judge a video by these two factors, since this is all we know before we view it, they can be misleading. What really matters is the quality of the content of the video.

....

Health claims on the front label of a food product may be the first thing we check when deciding whether to purchase it. Health claims describe a relationship between a food, food component, or dietary supplement and a disease or health-related condition. The Food and Drug Administration oversees determining which health claims may be used on the label of a food or dietary supplement.

Health claims can be abused and mislead the consumer, however. Cheerios have long been claiming to be heart healthy or to help lower your cholesterol because they are cholesterol-free, have less than a gram of saturated fat, and contain soluble fiber. But the FDA recently said in a letter to Cheerios that their new health claims were so outrageous that Cheerios would have to be sold as a cholesterol-reducing drug. Uh oh, Cheerios! You went too far with your health claims. (Plus, you are processed!)

When looking for real food, be wary of health claims, as they are often for marketing purposes only and should not carry a lot of weight when you determine if the food is high quality or not. It is really about the ingredients, and whether the food has undergone some serious processing!

youtube @youtube

#foodcovers

Searching for a song may lead you to a wannabe. Find the real deal, not someone pretending to be someone else. #foodcovers

For the best viewing experience, find the real deal, not someone pretending to be someone else. Seriously—if I type in the name of a song, I want to hear the actual artist singing it, not another 13-year-old girl singing it in front of her webcam, on her bed, guitar in lap. Get real.

....

Don't eat something pretending to be something else. What do I mean?

Foods Pretending To Be Something They're Not

Faux sugar: Saccharin, acesulfame-K, aspartame, and sucralose are examples of artificial sweeteners you may be familiar with. Research studies have shown links between artificial sweetener consumption and obesity, diabetes, and metabolic syndrome. Artificial sweeteners have also been defined as excitotoxins, affecting brain function. (Read more in the book *Excitotoxins: The Taste That Kills* by Russell Blaylock.) The great debate of whether a regular soda is better than a diet soda is essentially a question of the lesser of two evils. Without conclusive evidence, the best answer is to avoid both, since both are stresses on the body and are correlated with weight gain.

Faux fruit: The strawberries in Quaker Strawberries & Cream oatmeal are actually dehydrated apples (not strawberries) + artificial dye + artificial flavor. Tropicana adds unnatural flavor packs to make the taste consistent across all batches of a juice. Big-name food companies are playing up blueberries' known health benefits, but in reality their muffins and cereals don't contain any berries. Often these foods are just high fructose corn syrup, partially hydrogenated oils, and artificial flavors and colors. Consumers should read labels to see if blueberries are actually on the ingredients list, and be aware of the artificial colors that are used to fake the blueberries.

Faux meat: Fake meats such as veggie burgers and tofurkey are popular food choices among vegans who shun animal products. But unless it's organic, the soy that's a main source of protein in these products is often processed and extracted using hexane. According to the Centers for Disease Control, hexane is a neurotoxin, and I recommend avoiding it at all costs.

Eat the real thing (except for too much real sugar), not the harmful, chemical-laden wannabes.

youtube @youtube

#relatedfoods

Related Videos offer new suggestions that you will probably like. Thanks, YouTube! #relatedfoods

After viewing a YouTube video, Related Videos pop up to suggest similar types of uploads. If you liked the video you just watched, chances are you will like what YouTube is now suggesting. Don't ignore related videos, as they could lead to even more entertainment than the original video.

....

When making dietary changes, a safe approach is to make swaps with related foods to expand the list of foods you eat. Why should you do this? Variety is key, not only to maintaining a new way of eating, but to ensure that you are benefiting from all the different nutrients available in our real food supply. Here are some easy food swaps to increase the variety of nutrients in your diet.

- Peanut butter to other nut butters (almond, cashew)
- Iceberg or romaine lettuce to dark leafy greens, arugula, or kale
- Almonds to other nuts or seeds (ideally sprouted)
- Spaghetti to spaghetti squash
- Gluten-containing grains (pasta, bread) to gluten-free grains (rice, quinoa, corn)
- Canned tuna to canned salmon (salmon has lower mercury levels and is higher in omega-3s)
- Deli meats to fresh meats

youtube @youtube

#realfoodfavorites

Add high-quality videos to your Favorites for easy access. #realfoodfavorites

When you find a video you like, add it your Favorites! This will bookmark that video in your account so you can return to it easily for repeat viewing.

....

Just because Brussels sprouts are little nutrition cannon balls does not mean you should force yourself to eat them if you think they taste like dirty socks. As you incorporate new foods into your diet, keep track of favorites that you actually enjoy. No one said healthy eating has to taste disgusting! Plus, when you enjoy the flavor of real foods, it becomes a maintainable way of eating.

Once you've figured out what not to buy and also what is best to buy, develop a plan that will prevent you from relapsing into your old ways and the unhealthy comfort of a standard American diet. We all get stressed. We all become overworked. We all become tired. So it's important to have a backup plan, a repertoire of fast, easy, and simple foods that you can appreciate and that keep you from heading to the drive-thru.

youtube @youtube

#budgetfriendly

YouTube is free to use, so take advantage of this money-saving form of entertainment! #budgetfriendly

Getting a YouTube account is free and there is no limit to your amount of usage, so take advantage of all this money-saving entertainment. Hey, you can even use the savings to buy better-quality food!

The first money saver is with music. There probably isn't a song or a piece of a musical number that is publicly sold and not available on YouTube. Create playlists and enjoy free music. Take that a few steps further and think about how you could teach yourself new skills for free as well. There are cooking classes, technical assistance, car maintenance tips, and more. Beyond basic skills, learn how to cut or style your own hair, remodel your bedroom, or even garden!

Eating healthy costs too much? Lies. There are many ways to eat healthy on a budget. The first step is to reduce eating out at restaurants. You can really stretch your money when you cook at home and aren't paying the convenience factor (at the cost of quality!). Choose to buy your meats on sale, buy a whole chicken (organic) instead of breasts, and include beans and eggs as cheaper protein alternatives. Shop for produce that is in season or buy by the bag. Be conscious of where you can reap savings. Remember, the investment in your food is an investment in yourself. You are worth it!

youtube @youtube

#shoppinglist

Create a playlist to be used when you don't want to think about what to listen to next. #shoppinglist

Add individual videos to a playlist or create a new playlist by clicking the arrow next to the "Add to" button beneath the video. You can also easily convert your queue into a playlist and save it in your account so you can return to it later or share it with friends.

Creating a shopping list is a foolproof way to come home with the right choices for the week. Plus, there is no need to make impulse in-store decisions that can lead your eating habits down the drain. If you don't buy it, you won't eat it. Plan your week's meals, and buy only the foods you need. Your wallet and your tummy will thank you.

To get a free downloadable shopping list, please e-mail me at jenny@jennywesterkamp.com!

youtube @youtube

#viralfoods

Videos that go viral achieve extreme popularity, although whether they deserve it depends on the video. #viralfoods

Just putting a video on YouTube doesn't mean people will view it, talk about it, forward it, and be influenced by it. For a video to become viral, it needs to reach a certain threshold that might be considered a tipping point. Once it reaches this level of popularity, the number of views or "hits" spikes upward and the video becomes viral. This may happen when the video reaches YouTube's "Most Popular" list or is picked up and shown by a national news network.

Once this happens, the already-popular video gets even more publicity. Most viral videos are funny, short, authentic, and original. The intriguing thing about viral YouTube sensations is that they can make people popular quite quickly, but often their fame lasts for a short amount of time. Of course, there are successful YouTube sensations like Justin Bieber, and there are sure to be more.

....

Viral foods create sensations, sometimes deserved and sometimes not. PR firms, media campaigns, and celebrity endorsements can fuel the fire for these viral foods. Often they pique the interest of the public for a short time and then leave the spotlight shortly after. Like viral YouTube sensations, some deserve the popularity, while others simply do not. Even for those foods that deserve praise and attention, the media will often oversensationalize the food, promising a cure-all for a variety of health problems.

I don't believe that there is one food out there that has this power, but combining many powerful foods into a solid diet certainly is the way to go. Some certifiable viral foods of late include: pistachios, pomegranate, clementines (Cuties!), avocados, and coconut oil. Some unworthy viral foods include: high fructose corn syrup, agave nectar (which could also be categorized as a high fructose syrup), soy, and processed milk. Got milk? No thanks.

youtube @youtube

#promotedfoods

Promoted videos are typically more like commercials, and less entertaining. #promotedfoods

When initially searching for a video, look to channels or videos that are created by a credible, unbiased source. Always look at the credibility of the advice given. A safe rule is to be sure that the information is not coming from someone who can make money off of your attention.

....

If it is advertised on TV, it is probably not good for you. For example, you read about how high fructose corn syrup (HFCS) is really just another sugar, but the Corn Refiners Association that produces HFCS is paying for that message! Only 5% of food advertising is for real whole foods, and the rest is for processed foods and alcohol. Food companies with big advertising budgets succeed (and very well, for that matter) at selling inexpensive, calorically dense foods that are not nutritionally dense.

You may have a hard time stepping away from this advertising and listening to your body and what you are truly craving: real food! When you are constantly bombarded with images of processed foods (whether you consciously know it or not), probability is against you for what you will first turn to when you are hungry. Fight against this probability and know when a food is being promoted not for its nutrients but for its profit.

youtube @youtube

#GMOs

Don't mess with human nature's ability to entertain. #GMOs

For me, the most hilarious videos on YouTube are the laughing babies. I laugh so hard that I cry. And not just the first time I see it, but *every* time I see it. Humans create great entertainment just in everyday situations. A recent viral video included a proposal to a girl through a lip-synced music video. YouTube is able to spread that real human entertainment to the masses. This makes us feel good inside! It makes us feel human.

We don't need to travel so far away from simple day-to-day occurrences in order to savor life's moments. Often we want more activity, more excitement, and we want it now. Slow down and understand there are exciting things happening all around you. Get out your phone camera and capture it. And then upload it for all to see.

....

Not to be a downer, but I think genetically modified organisms (GMOs) might end the human race. GMOs are created when a gene from one species is transferred to another, creating something that would not be found in nature. In food, GMOs are crop plants created for human or animal consumption that have been modified in the laboratory to produce higher yields, contain more vitamins and minerals, or resist insect and plant diseases. That's good, right? Wrong.

In America, 85% of corn, canola, sugar beets, and soybeans are grown from GMO seed. That translates to 80% of conventional processed grocery store food containing a GMO. GMOs are bad for your body, bad for the community, bad for farmers, and bad for the environment. They have never been tested for long-term effects on health, and can cause allergic reactions, resistance to antibiotics, and reproductive problems.

Consumers worry about the safety of GMOs and are working to get all GMO food labeled in the United States, just as they are already in many countries around the world. Food suppliers did have good intentions—to be able to feed the world more cheaply—but we have to realize that we can't mess with nature as much as we have. We know the road to hell was paved with good intentions. We have to get back to the basics of human survival.

GMOs have only been in our food supply for fifteen years and most of us eat them every day. Critics are saying it's time for change. Anyone else seen significant increases in cancer, autoimmune disease, food sensitivities since then? These types of food situations are things that should make you go "hmmmm."

To Limit Your Exposure to GMOs

- Buy fresh, local, and 100% certified organic foods
- Avoid processed foods, especially corn- and soy-based foods
- Download the free shopping guide from www.nongmoshoppingguide.com or the ShopNoGMO iPhone app
- Read the books by Jeffrey Smith: *Seeds of Deception: Exposing Industry and Government Lies About the Safety of the Genetically Engineered Foods You're Eating* (Fairfield, Iowa: Yes! Books, 2003) and *Genetic Roulette: The Documented Health Risks of Genetically Engineered Foods*, (Fairfield, Iowa: Yes! Books, 2007)
- Sign petitions against GMOs at fooddemocracynow.org

#summary #youtube

Simplify your search for real entertainment and get back to true human experience. Be wary of wannabes and promoted videos. #summary #youtube

#summary #findrealfood

Simplify your search for real food and get back to connecting with your food. Be wary of fake food and profit. #summary #findrealfood

FOURSQUARE MEALS

foursquare @foursquare

#localfood

Foursquare was the first location-driven social media app, using GPS technology. #localfood

Foursquare's distinguishing factor is that it's all about location. Whether using an iPhone, Blackberry, or Android, Foursquare users can "check in" at various locations and connect with friends through their smartphone. This social networking tool uses the GPS in mobile devices to link up with the locations that users visit—favorite restaurants, bars, or stores—and connects the users to Twitter and Facebook.

Foursquare users earn points and badges each time they visit a particular location, and if a user checks in to a venue on more days than anyone else in the previous 60 days, that user will be named the "mayor" of the venue. Certain venues use the point system or "mayorship" as a marketing tactic for discounts or daily specials to increase visits by their clientele. As of September 2012, Foursquare reported over 25 million users and over 3 million check-ins per day.

Buy local, go local, eat local. We've all heard phrases involving "local" and our food supply around the water cooler or at the supermarket. Buying local means selecting foods grown close to your home. But how close is close? The average distance "fresh" produce travels before being consumed is 1,500 miles.

Eating local depends on your geographic region and population density, but it is much less than that, about 100 miles or so. The benefits of going local include supporting the nearby farming economy, knowing the environment your food was grown in, and reducing energy cost in food transportation. The less the food travels, the less energy it needs, and the more sustainable it is for the environment.

Even if you are eating organic produce from the grocery

store, it is likely that this food traveled thousands of miles, going through many stops between the farm and your kitchen table. Think of the exhaust and pollution its travel creates on its journey. By choosing to eat food based on its closer location, you will reap many benefits in addition to helping out the environment.

foursquare @foursquare

#supportlocaleconomy

By checking in at your community's businesses, you can support the local economy. #supportlocaleconomy

Foursquare supports local businesses by allowing them to use free tools for tracking customer traffic (including real-time analytics and social reach information), which can be a source of valuable information. Merchants can share updates about what's happening at their location when their best customers are nearby, and Foursquare helps new people find them. As a Foursquare user, you should not hesitate to check in at these local businesses and support their efforts in your community.

....

Money spent with local farmers, growers, and artisans all stays close to home, working to build your local economy instead of being handed over to a corporation in another city, state, or country. In another way, since the food moves through fewer entities, more of the money you spend tends to get straight to the people growing locally.

foursquare @foursquare

#createcommunity

Expand your community, meet new people, and develop new relationships. #createcommunity

As a Foursquare user, you can share or read other users' tips and recommendations. This information sharing is a great way to create community, as you can meet other people who are frequenting the same places as you. Chatting about your favorite dishes, things to do, how to get a discount, and even where to find clean bathrooms, everyone in your community benefits. It's a win-win for all!

....

Local food creates community because you are able to connect with "the hand that feeds you." Instead of knowing the person who bags your groceries at your local supermarket, you can now know the one who is picking your apple off the tree. The beauty of this is that you can talk directly to the people growing your food. You can ask if they use pesticides or fertilizers, and if they spray the fruits and vegetables directly or just spray the plant early in the season. Many local farmers offer organic produce, which is obviously the best choice, but sometimes small farms cannot pay the big bucks for the official organic certification; they still use minimal fertilizers, and only before the crop appears. Beyond the farmer, you can develop closer connections to vendors at the farmers' market, the local cheese shop, your favorite butcher, or a co-op that sells local eggs. Here you can easily meet new people interested in eating locally.

Go a step further and volunteer at your local farmers' market, plant a community garden, or donate some real food to your food bank. The local food movement depends on everyone taking part in it, expanding the community and developing new relationships.

foursquare @foursquare

#betterforyou

Foursquare is meant to enhance in-person social experiences, and one way of doing this is through Lists. #betterforyou

You may think you live within the bubble of the social media world on your phone, but Foursquare is meant to enhance in-person social experiences in the world around you. Lists are collections of tips and venues created by users. They help you find the best of anything! There are many lists, ranging from "Best Museums of Chicago" to "Best Hot Dog Joints." Each list is typically created by users who consider themselves as local experts, giving a unique perspective into their city.

You can find new lists to follow within the app (tap the "Lists" tab) or on Foursquare's Lists Discovery page. If you have an iPhone, Foursquare's Radar feature can remind you when you're near a spot that's on one of the lists you follow.

....

Local food is fresher and tastes better, and is better for you! Taste lettuce that was picked yesterday versus lettuce picked last week. You can tell the difference. To be sold in a store, produce is often picked before it ripens so that by the time it reaches its destination thousands of miles away, it will be ripe. On the other hand, local food is as fresh as you can find it, still with rich flavor and all of its nutrients and enzymes intact. As a living food, produce begins to lose its benefits with time. It may also be waxed to make it look pretty and ripe. Tomatoes are often gassed to make them ripen faster. Local produce naturally ripens in the ground and is fresh for the eating! Finally, from a safety standpoint, the fewer steps there are between your food's source and your table, the less chance there is of contamination. In conclusion, it is better for you!

foursquare @foursquare

#exploreyouroptions

Explore options and take advantage of the world around you. #exploreyouroptions

The Explore option provides recommendations that take into account the weather, time of day, your location, and your friends' activities. Use this technology to your advantage in order to find new spots around you that you never knew existed.

....

If you never considered eating locally, it is time to explore your options.

> *Farmers' markets:* Farmers' markets typically run outdoors April through October, although in some places they may start earlier in the year and close later, and some markets run year round and/or indoors. Local farmers gather at a certain time and location one or more days each week to sell directly to the people in their community. The foods usually include fruits and vegetables, and often cheeses, meats, eggs and dairy, and baked goods.
>
> *Community Supported Agriculture (CSAs):* CSAs are becoming increasingly popular. Farmers begin before planting by selling "shares" (or memberships) to the public. You're basically buying a portion of the output of the farm. During the growing season, you receive a box of food the farm has produced each week. It might be delivered right to your front door, or you might pick it up from a location near you. All you have to do is open your box and begin enjoying the local food with no hassle. A share usually consists of produce and may also include flowers, eggs, and other farm products. The perk of a

CSA is the variety that you can get, since most CSA boxes are a surprise each time, depending on how well the crops grew!

The easiest way to find a CSA is to search localharvest.org, which lists thousands of CSAs across the United States. Before purchasing a CSA share, it's important to consider if a farm is organic or follows organic standards, the cost, the delivery options, and box sizes. Starting with a smaller share may be better if you do not cook a lot or are not sure if all the produce would be used before it spoils.

foursquare @foursquare

#deals

Getting deals with companies is a great perk of being an active Foursquare user. #deals

There are several ways that check-ins can "unlock" a reward to receive a special at a venue. As provided by Foursquare, the types of unlocking deals include:

Mayor: especially for the standing mayor
Newbie: unlocked on your first check-in at that place
Swarm: check in with a massive group of people
Friends: check in with the 'x' number of friends
Flash: the wildcard of the specials world—you never know when one will pop up!
Check-in, Frequency, Loyalty: check in 'x' number of times

In the same way, there are ways to get deals when eating locally.

- Develop a relationship with farmer, and if you are a consistent customer, he or she may offer discounts or extras.
- Receive specials when placing your first order with a co-op or CSA.
- Go in on group discounts with bulk purchasing.
- At the end of the market day, some vendors may sell their remaining fresh items at a discount.

foursquare @foursquare

#setgoals

Badges, while seemingly unimportant, are motivation to check in frequently and be more active on the site. #setgoals

Badges are a fun reward for checking in a certain number of times or at certain places. Some badges can only be earned in a specific city. When a user gains a badge, he or she has the same badge across all cities, and the badge will remain on that user's profile indefinitely. A handful of introductory badges are earned as milestones in usage. Some badges are tied to venue "tags" and the badge earned depends on the tags applied to the venue. Other badges may be specific to a city, venue, event, or date.

Examples of badges include: Superstar (checking in at 50 different venues), Player Please! (checking in along with three or more of the opposite sex in one night), and Crunked! (checking in at four or more spots in one night).

....

When becoming a "locavore," you can aim to set goals for yourself so that you are consistent in your local eating endeavors. For example, you might try one new type of produce each week, or devote a certain percentage of your food budget to local eating. If you aren't able to fill up your menu with home-cooked local foods, choose to identify and support a restaurant that serves locally sourced foods.

Setting goals and achieving those goals will keep your motivation high and will be rewarding in the long run. While you benefit from being a locavore, you are benefiting the world around you, and you should feel really good about that, perhaps enough to make yourself a badge to wear!

foursquare @foursquare

#variety

Rack up your Foursquare points, and see where you stand among your friends. #variety

Each time you check in, Foursquare awards you points. Every check-in earns at least one point, with bonus points awarded for certain things like being the mayor, checking in with a new friend, or checking in on certain holidays. The points don't really do anything, but they're fun to give you an idea where you stand against your friends.

Action	Points Earned
Checking in to a new place	5 points
Adding a new venue	5 points
Being the first of the user's friends to check into a new location	3 points
Checking in to a place the user has been before	1 point
Location multiplier for each place a user goes in a day	1 point per location
Points for checking in with the same friend at multiple locations	BFF bonus

The point system in Foursquare helps you to keep adding variety to the places you explore. In the same way, local foods create greater variety of foods available because they don't all have to be just the few standard items that the store knows will sell well. Having the support and demand from their community, farmers at CSAs and farmers' markets can grow a larger variety of crops—for example, heritage tomatoes or apples—than what is available at your grocery store. Take advantage of this variety by trying something new!

foursquare @foursquare

#perksofconsistency

Become the mayor of a venue by checking in more than anyone else in the previous 60 days to receive extra perks. #perksofconsistency

Everyone knows you really love a place when you visit enough times to be the mayor. You'll get recognized on the venue's Foursquare profile page and other users will see your picture when they check in. (You must have a profile picture in order to be named mayor of a venue.) Even after you've been named mayor, you must continuously check in to maintain your position. You then get special mayor deals at that venue. FYI: Someone else may earn the title next by checking in more times than you, and you would lose your mayorship perks.

Eating locally must be done consistently for you to see the benefits. The more you incorporate local foods into your diet, the more you get out of it. Working directly with a farmer, connecting with your community, experiencing the seasonality of different foods throughout the year, and benefiting from their superior flavor and freshness make for great perks of consistency.

#summary #foursquare

Connect with local businesses, support your local economy, and make a positive impact on your life and community. #summary #foursquare

#summary #eatlocally

Connect with local farmers, support local food, and make a positive impact on your health and community. #summary #eatlocally

in

GET LINKEDIN
MY BELLY

linkedin @linkedin

#whysupplement

You can't ignore that you need LinkedIn. #whysupplement

There is simply no way to ignore the power of LinkedIn. With over 80 million users and a new user added every second, LinkedIn is the best professional social networking site for business people and job seekers. What is unique about LinkedIn is that it has a much higher quality of users, with a higher average household income per member, than any other social network. Of note, every Fortune 500 company is represented! In your professional career, there will come a time when you need a connection. LinkedIn is where you can cultivate these connections, because you never know when you will need them.

Often referred to as "Facebook for professionals," LinkedIn serves as a way for people to maintain different details and information on their contacts as well as network within their profession. LinkedIn has many benefits for both employers and job seekers. Employers can post jobs and look up potential candidates, while job seekers can research companies, locate hiring managers to look for mutual connections, and job-search through job postings, professional affiliations, and recruitment initiatives. With more effort required to sustain a presence, LinkedIn ends up being the forgotten network for many of us, and most of us majorly underutilize its power since we simply think "I don't need this." News flash! You can't ignore this social network.

Our "standard American diet" (SAD!) is very low in minerals, too low in healthy fats, and high in refined carbohydrates. Dr. Michael Roizen, who helped write Dr. Mehmet Oz's books, said that of the two and a half million Americans whose diets were examined for nutrient adequacy, only 0.1% had such good diets that they didn't need vitamin or mineral supplementation. Processed foods lack key nutrients that are vital for energy, muscle, healing, and overall health. In addition, the soil that our food is grown in is depleted of nutrients due to overfarming, so the the nutrient content of fruits and vegetables has gone down with it (the soil is where the plants get nutrients).

We are starting to understand the power of supplementation on top of a solid real food diet. According to the National Institutes of Health, interest in and usage of complementary and alternative medicine (CAM), which includes supplementation, is increasing. With this newfound interest, we see a boom in the nutrition supplement industry. Fifty percent of Americans now take a multivitamin.

The first step is understanding that you need to ward off nutrient deficiencies, and smart supplementation is a way to do this. The key is to focus on quality whole food supplements, in addition to a real food diet, and realize that not all supplements are created equal.

linkedin @linkedin

#supplementuses

Determine how you want to use LinkedIn. #supplementuses

You can benefit from this professional social network through research, education, brand management, and relationship building. For research, you can search profiles and see who's doing what, or learn about potential employers and customers. Educationally speaking, there are networking and business events, webinars, and seminars to take advantage of. When creating your brand or image, you can control how you portray yourself or your service to others. Finally, in relationship building, you can take your connections to the next level with messages, recommendations, and introductions. Determine how you want to use LinkedIn, whether for all these or only focusing on one, and you can take your professional life to the next level.

....

There are many uses for supplementation. Working with athletes, I find their reasons for supplementation include better performance, injury prevention, faster recovery, and stress support. Other general uses for supplementation include preventing or correcting nutrient deficiencies, supporting stress management in a high-stress world, and dealing with acute health issues.

linkedin @linkedin

#paynoworpaylater

The amount of time you put into LinkedIn may not pay off now, but will likely pay off later. #paynoworpaylater

Simply by creating a LinkedIn profile, you improve your findability on a Google search so potential connections can find you. Remember that search engines will pick up your LinkedIn page, so if someone is looking specifically for you, they might well find that first. Spend a little time on this, and make sure that you've got your key messages right. Once you have done this, you must maintain your presence on the network and continue to grow. Your résumé should be changing at all times. If you have an active online presence—which you should—your connections should be growing as well as your experience. This takes time and upkeep.

Many users set up their profile and don't update it for years. Lots of people join LinkedIn because they receive an invitation from someone. But they don't go on to make the most of LinkedIn because they're busy, or they don't understand how it could be useful to them. You are wasting potential opportunities for professional growth later on down the road. LinkedIn offers so many tools for selling yourself, it would be silly not to take advantage of this platform. Making your professional experience and contact information easily accessible on LinkedIn will give you a greater chance to get noticed or get hired.

Avoiding nutrient deficiencies is a difficult task. What's worse, it is hard to detect if you are deficient in certain nutrients unless you have symptoms (your body's signal telling you that it is not working properly). As with connections, you never know when you will need one for a new business opportunity. In times of stress, the body needs more ammunition. Making sure that you are filling your nutrient quotas through a whole foods diet and smart supplementation may not seem like you will benefit immediately, but in terms of prevention you are going a long way. An ounce of prevention IS worth a pound of cure.

The nutritional content in our food system has dropped dramatically over the last 100 years. Erosion, overuse of fertilizers, and other poor farming practices have left soil and food depleted of essential nutrients and microorganisms. When we factor in hectic lifestyles, daily stress, poor social eating habits, strenuous athletic activities, and alcohol intake, the personal picture becomes even grimmer. While your diet should always form the critical foundation for optimal health and wellness, carefully selected supplementation guided by a trained health professional is ideal.

linkedin @linkedin

#dietisfoundation

Build your profile to full completion. #dietisfoundation

Go for 100% completion on your profile page so you are ready to make things happen! Your profile page can list your education, past work history, current and past projects, groups and associations, and more. Choose your words carefully, knowing that your manager or supervisor, as well as all your contacts, will be able to access the information.

One area that is repeatedly neglected on the profile is the photograph. This is a necessity and increases your ability to be contacted by the right people. Business apparel for some is best and business casual is a minimum requirement. Look friendly, smart, and approachable. This is your first impression on LinkedIn.

Another area of your profile to complete is your 120-character headline, which sits at the top of your profile and describes who you are and how you can help. Here is where you need to use brief, descriptive, compelling keywords so the right professionals can discover you. Then complete your work history and education information. If you have a website, be sure to customize your listing by choosing the "Other" option to use a more descriptive phrase for the link. Finally, include a link to your Twitter profile. LinkedIn will let you know when you have reached 100% completion!

....

Supplements are meant to complete your diet. If they were meant to replace your diet, they would be called "replacements," right? Without a solid diet of real food, supplements are not going to take your health to the next level. You lose the potential power of supplements when you have a poor diet. As with having a poor, incomplete LinkedIn profile, adding extra nutrient connections to your diet will not give the same return on investment if you aren't ready for them. Nutrients won't be utilized or digested as well; it will not be worth the money and time required to take them. If, on the other hand, you do have a complete real food diet, adding supplementation to the mix can greatly improve your health and support your goals in wellness and disease prevention.

linkedin @linkedin

#nutrientconnections

Add your connections to your LinkedIn profile. #nutrientconnections

Connections are to LinkedIn what friends are to Facebook: other registered users you know personally. It's time to be proactive and invite connections to your LinkedIn profile. Although you can invite anyone to be a connection, they will need to set up an account to use the site. You can invite people to become a connection and be invited yourself.

Don't wait to be invited, though—if you believe someone could be beneficial to you, you would genuinely like to connect with them on a deeper level, or just find them really interesting, send that invitation out. There are many ways to add connections and LinkedIn makes it super easy.

- Import your address book from your e-mail and send appropriate people invitations, using the "Add Connections" feature.
- Review the "People You May Know" list. This is LinkedIn's connection suggestion engine!
- Search people or companies of interest using the "Search" feature.

Once you have connected and they are added to your network, you can review background information on them and view their connections as well. Finding out that you have something in common or have a mutual connection makes the connection that much stronger. Plus, you never know when you will need this connection in the future.

There are over 90 essential nutrients in the body. Nutrients, like connections, are important to have on board, whether we need them now or later. There are many different kinds of nutrients, and nutrition scientists are learning more and more about each one. The saying that applies here is: "The more we know, the more we realize we don't know."

Nutrition is still a relatively new science, so we are still understanding the many roles that a single nutrient could play in the body. Instead of waiting for new research on the next supernutrient, supplementation with a wide spectrum of food-based nutrients is a commonsense and safe approach, knowing that we are not going too far from nature by doing this. Nutrients have more roles than we even realize, and a deficiency of any one of the essential nutrients can lead to chronic diseases. Start inviting those nutrient connections.

linkedin @linkedin

#wholefoodsupplements

It's all about who you know. Only invite those to connect whom you actually know. #wholefoodsupplements

"It is not what you know, but who you know." Your strongest connections will be those with people you have met face to face and know well. Usually these are college friends, colleagues, partners, clients, friends, or family. By connecting with them on LinkedIn, you can see what they are up to in their professional lives and help them easily when they need it—or vice versa. As you get to know more people in person, do not hesitate to send them a LinkedIn invitation shortly after meeting to maintain the relationship.

Whole food supplements supply your body with nutrients you are not getting from your diet—all the vitamins, minerals, trace minerals, and phytonutrients that foods possess—in a way that nature intended, with the same molecular structure as found in real food. Whole food supplements work on the basis that your body knows and will recognize nutrients better if they come from food concentrates.

Not only are you getting extra nutrients from food, but when processed correctly, supplements include a variety of the plant's components that will work synergistically to provide the best results. This allows you to build on a strong foundational diet, especially when you are already eating several servings of fruits and vegetables each day. Stick with whole food supplements, such as food-based essential fatty acids, green drinks, or food-based multivitamins that your body will know and recognize to support your healthy lifestyle.

linkedin @linkedin

#syntheticsupplements

Avoid connecting with random people whom you don't really know. #syntheticsupplements

There is a negative connotation with connecting on LinkedIn with people you don't know, and the site takes many steps to prevent this from happening. For example, you may be asked to provide the e-mail address of a person you want to connect with, in order to prove that you have had communication outside of LinkedIn.

For good reason, many people are selective about whom they accept as a connection on LinkedIn, so it's risky to try to connect with randoms. You, too, should be wary of accepting invitations to connect when you do not know the person. However, there's nothing wrong with looking at peoples' profiles to see their work history, interests, and education background to see if there is a potential for a relationship.

There are many different kinds of supplements on the market, and it can be very confusing to determine the true value of a supplement. Synthetic supplements can take longer for your body to process; they may leave behind by-products and trace toxic compounds that can damage your health in the long run.

We often think "more is better" when choosing supplements, but quality is far more important than quantity. A small amount of a vitamin in whole food form can be far more effective than a large dose of an isolated vitamin. In addition, some people are allergic to the base of the synthetics, which may consist of petrochemical derivatives, nicotine, and coal tars (by-products of coal).

Most synthetic vitamins and supplements are chemical compounds that cannot be found in nature, so the human body does not recognize these ingredients. Hypervitaminosis (high storage levels of vitamins) can more likely occur from a "pure, isolated" compound, as the body may recognize it not as food but as a toxin. It is best to avoid synthetic supplements and megadoses of any isolated nutrients.

linkedin @linkedin

#qualitysupplements

It's not the number of connections but the quality of the relationships that you have developed with these connections. #qualitysupplements

All LinkedIn connections should be realistic candidates for professional relationships. When you link up with another LinkedIn user, the potential should exist for your partnership to blossom. Don't waste time connecting with those unrelated to your professional goals, and instead focus on a clear and clean list of contacts. Again, more is not better. It's better to have 50 solid contacts rather than thousands of people you don't actually know.

....

The unavoidable problem with supplements is that their quality is not well regulated. For me, this is especially a problem when suggesting supplements to professional athletes. Supplement manufacturers are not required to provide evidence supporting the efficacy of their products, so some may take advantage of this lack of transparency, resulting in consistency issues and questions about their sources and forms of nutrients in the product.

What's more dangerous is that the potency and purity of extractions can vary. Cheap additives can significantly affect absorption and metabolism as well. Toxic agents may be added to the product or sneaky substitutions made in order to save money. Buyer beware!

linkedin @linkedin

#supplementdangers

Watch out for people offering too-good-to-be-true business opportunities. #supplementdangers

When you are sent a message to connect, the potential connection could you make an irresistible offer to work with them or give you an opportunity that makes you feel special and highly sought after. They make you feel like you are special, but unless you already know this person, they are likely not a high-quality connection. Only if you can vouch for their credibility through a shared connection should those "exciting business opportunities" be taken seriously. It is likely that they are contacting tens if not hundreds of other people in your field offering the same proposal. Would you randomly ask someone you didn't know to be a part of a million-dollar idea? Probably not.

In the flurry of the misleading promotion and false supplement claims, multilevel marketing (MLM) supplements take the gluten free cake as too-good-to-be-true solutions for you. MLM products often use the same bulk ingredients as products available in traditional stores, but are more costly due to their labor-intensive business model. This encourages sellers to say that the MLM products are better than others. Sellers may even go beyond the official claims represented in the product literature with their testimonials. Government regulation is hard to enforce, as it requires agencies such as the Federal Trade Commission (FTC) to devote already inadequate resources to collecting evidence, and the number of MLM false claims and frauds greatly exceeds their capacity to prosecute. Watch out for dangerous and too-good-to-be-true claims.

linkedin @linkedin

#professionalrecommendations

Get recommendations for public endorsement of your work. #professionalrecommendations

Whether you are looking for a job, changing careers, or simply working on your career management, ask for recommendations from past coworkers, supervisors, and other connections you have done business with. The Recommendations feature allows people who've worked together in an organization or on a project to endorse one another. Recommendations will appear on your profile after the reference submits their commentary, usually a paragraph or two.

Having at least three recommendations solidifies your skills and shows potential connections that people value your work and think of you in a positive light. How do you get Recommendations? Ask! On your profile page, click on the "Get Recommended" link and fill in the form it takes you to. Again, don't be shy! If the feature's there, you might as well use it!

When possible, I like to use whole food–based supplements from professional-grade companies, manufactured at NSF- and Good Manufacturing Practices (GMP)–certified facilities. If a supplement is certified under the United States Pharmacopeial Convention (USP) or by NSF International or the United Natural Products Alliance, it's guaranteed to meet a certain standard of quality, although synthetic supplements may carry these labels as well.

It is difficult, as a consumer, to decide where to get high-quality supplements, so I suggest always consulting with a healthcare professional trained in supplementation (like me!).

linkedin @linkedin

#overdosing

Even though LinkedIn defaults to adding all e-mail contacts on LinkedIn, do not automatically add them all. #overdosing

When you go to add connections on your LinkedIn profile, you will be prompted to share your e-mail contact list. This will then generate a list of LinkedIn users who were on your contact list. LinkedIn defaults to selecting all contacts to add, but really, you should be building your network with a purpose. Not every person that you have ever e-mailed deserves an invitation, and a person who does deserve one may not appreciate an automated one. It is possible to overdose on the invites. Be purposeful with each one.

....

What you really need supplementation for is to build up nutrient stores to counter diet deficiencies, based on your current situation. Overdosing on certain nutrients without understanding what that can do to your body is dangerous. Buying a supplement and taking high doses can produce some scary results. Vitamin B_6 overdose can lead to tingling and numbing of limbs. Vitamin D overdose (seen at 430 times the recommended amount) is associated with mental retardation and heart defects. Too much of a good thing is no longer a good thing when it comes to isolated nutrients found in supplementation. Be purposeful and safe with each one you take.

linkedin @linkedin

#watersolublevitamins

Coworkers are connections who may change throughout your career, with either you or them changing jobs. #watersolublevitamins

Coworkers, both past and present, can be an easy way to start building your network. You start by entering your employment history and attaching your account to the companies for whom you have worked. By visiting your company's page, you can review a list of all employees and can add them to your network. In addition, LinkedIn will show a list titled "Just Joined LinkedIn" at the bottom of your homepage to allow you to connect to any new coworkers who join. Coworkers come and go as you or they move on to different companies or positions. Their value fluctuates because of this. For what it's worth, they are at least people you know personally, so will always be a strong connection.

Water-soluble vitamins are beneficial in the body, and we need a continuous supply of them in our diets. They are used in our body to varying degrees, and anything not used is removed from the body via urine output, rather than stored. Water-soluble vitamins are the B-complex group and vitamin C. The exception to excretion is vitamin B_{12}, which your body can store in your liver for years.

linkedin @linkedin

#fatsolublevitamins

Classmates are connections you share an undying bond with that will never leave. #fatsolublevitamins

You can connect to classmates in a similar manner to coworkers. Once you enter your education information on your LinkedIn profile, it will automatically add your classmates to the list of people you may know. In addition, LinkedIn will include your classmates in the "Just Joined LinkedIn" list along with colleagues. The value of connecting with classmates stays relatively the same throughout your career, since your education does not change the way your jobs may. Like coworkers, classmates are valuable connections because you know them well.

Fat-soluble nutrients can be stored in the body; it is not vital to consume them every day. When you have more than your body needs on any given day, the excess will be stored, unlike water-soluble nutrients that are generally excreted. The fat-soluble vitamins are A, D, E, and K. Consuming these fat-soluble vitamins with a fat source helps their absorption. For example, adding avocado or nuts to a salad will allow you to absorb the vitamin A of the other vegetables in the salad.

linkedin @linkedin

#macrominerals

Connect with LinkedIn users whom you know and who have large networks. #macrominerals

Connect with people who have many connections in the field, because this will expand your network of second- and third-degree connections. Keep reaching out and networking!

....

Calcium, sulfur, sodium, potassium, phosphorus, chlorine, and magnesium make up the macrominerals, which have a large variety of functions in the body, including bone and teeth formation, cell growth and repair, and energy metabolism. By continually making sure you have enough of these nutrients on board, you can be sure that many functions in the body will run smoothly.

linkedin @linkedin

#traceminerals

Connect with a few LinkedIn users who are at the top of your field. #traceminerals

Connections with a few high-profile professionals in your field may be all you need to improve the credibility of your profile and get found more easily. Ideally, you will have a shared connection with them, or have met them in person or by e-mail before approaching them on LinkedIn.

....

Don't forget about zinc, copper, iron, manganese, iodine, cobalt, fluoride, and selenium. While you need less of them, trace minerals are still vital, and play a very active role in the body, especially in detoxification, digestion, and thyroid health.

linkedin @linkedin

#essentialfattyacids

Connect with gurus who provide mentally stimulating information, to educate yourself in your field. #essentialfattyacids

LinkedIn users are able to post updates as often as they'd like and there are many who take the reins to provide their connections with highly relatable and valuable information on a near-daily basis. Identifying these connections is like finding an informational gold mine, as you now have a great source as you delve deeper into your specialization or field.

Essential fatty acids (EFAs) are a family of lipids (fats) important to health, especially to the health of the brain. The primary essential fatty acids are omega-3 (alpha-linolenic acid) and omega-6 (linoleic acid). Of the two primary fatty acids, omega-3 can be further divided into two related essential fatty acids, docosahexaenoic acid (DHA) and eicosapentaenoic acid (EPA). DHA is the predominant fatty acid in cells and the primary fat in the human brain, with small amounts of EPA also present. DHA can also be converted back to EPA if needed.

Good supplement sources of EFAs are evening primrose oil, safflower oil, sunflower oil, black currant oil, and currant seed oil.

linkedin @linkedin

#lifecycleneeds

Join different LinkedIn groups, depending on your needs at the time. #lifecycleneeds

Have you joined any groups in LinkedIn? As a member of a LinkedIn group, you can see the group's member list and potentially use it to develop additional LinkedIn connections. Join groups that are relevant to your business and target markets. Consider joining alumni groups, peer groups, and groups that are organized around the professional and personal topics you are most interested in. Lastly, think about groups where your target markets might be hanging out, so you can find ways to be creatively visible and valuable to them with the resources and insights you share.

Share relevant, resourceful, rich content with your groups that can help other members. Ask questions and respond to comments!

When you fall into different life cycles, you have different nutrient needs as well. During growth spurts, pregnancy, infection, intense activity, illness, high stress, trauma, or recovery from surgery, as your nutrient needs increase you'll gain much benefit with supplementing. For example, during adolescence, there is an increased need for iron, calcium, zinc, and B vitamins, as these are essential for growth and development. During pregnancy, supplementing with folic acid, iron, magnesium, and vitamin B_{12} are important for supporting healthy fetal development. In high stress, vitamin C, B vitamins, and magnesium are especially needed.

linkedin @linkedin

#nutrientdeficiencies

Get back in touch with people.
#nutrientdeficiencies

Why do you want to get back in touch with people with whom you've lost touch? Well, these are people who could be in your network, but aren't. One of the primary uses of a tool like LinkedIn is to give you a good excuse to get back in touch with the people you've not spoken to in a while. They're people who could be telling other people about you and what you do, or could be out there looking for opportunities for you, but because you've lost touch with them, they're probably not sure of what you're doing or don't think about you when something comes up that you'd like to hear about.

Most business opportunities come through networking, so you need to make sure that your network is as wide as you can make it. One of the best ways of doing this is by getting involved again with people with whom you've already made a connection.

Chronic diseases are a result of a chronic nutrient deficiency. Spotting the physical signs not of a "normal part of aging" but of a potential nutrient deficiency, you can address the deficiency and prevent the problems that come along with it by supplementing with those nutrients and improving your diet. Get back in touch with all your essential nutrients! (See "Physical Signs of Nutrient Deficiencies" in the Appendix.)

linkedin @linkedin

#cofactornutrients

Make use of Introductions to gain critical connections. #cofactornutrients

Introductions occur when a third party brings together two people who aren't currently connected. Your connections combine in ways that you don't even realize, so it is hard to know where each one will lead. First-, second-, and third-degree connections will continue to surprise you as your relationship progresses. Introductions, either given or received, can spark a new opportunity, but if you don't use this feature, you won't know what you are missing.

....

Cofactors are components that are needed for a nutrient to work properly. Without this link, the nutrient's function suffers. There are many intricate relationships among nutrients, but here are some examples of how one nutrient makes the introduction for another.

Zinc is a cofactor for protein digestion and insulin activity.
Vitamin C is a cofactor for iron absorption.
Magnesium is a cofactor for calcium absorption.
Copper is a cofactor for iron utilization.
Carnitine is a cofactor for iron, vitamin C, B_3, and B_6.
Iodine is a cofactor for oxidative reactions in thyroid functioning.
Manganese is a cofactor for protein synthesis.
Protein, magnesium, zinc, B_6, and B_{12} are cofactors for metabolic utilization of EFAs.

See how each nutrient can make an introduction for another to allow it to reach its potential in your body? Amazing!

linkedin @linkedin

#fatlosssupport

Find the connection that can get you to the next level. #fatlosssupport

A connection who can get you to the next level is one you quickly want to identify if looking for a promotion, job advancement, or a new business opportunity. Search out the centers of influence—connections with large networks and a lot of recommendations, both given and received. They might also engage in groups and use LinkedIn consistently. Basically, they are bomb LinkedIn users, so they are probably bomb in real life, and by getting to know them, you can take your professional life to the next level.

....

Fat loss, assuming you are above a normal body fat percentage, will take you to the next level in wellness. By especially reducing waist circumference (which is connected to chronic diseases), you should aim for normal body composition (see #bodycomposition in Breakfast Lunch & Twitter). Fat loss can be difficult to achieve, and supplementation of key fat-loss nutrients in addition to a solid diet and exercise regimen can push you to a healthier body composition.

L-carnitine: Supports the body's utilization of fat for fuel

Chromium picolinate: Helps prevent the loss of lean body mass while losing fat, and helps keep blood sugar stable by improving insulin sensitivity and reducing cravings

Conjugated linoleic acid (CLA): A fatty acid that research shows may help burn abdominal fat

E-mail me at jenny@jennywesterkamp.com for my best fat loss tips!

linkedin @linkedin

#stresssupport

Friends and family connections are great to have around when you are really in need. #stresssupport

While you may think family and friends are for Facebook or Twitter, they may actually be your strongest LinkedIn connections when you are under stress. They are most willing to help you, especially in dire situations such as looking for a new job or connecting with an important person needed to close a deal. I have connected with several family members and have been surprised to find out that my business contacts know members of my family. It really is a small world!

....

Stress occurs daily. Nutrients are used up more quickly when you're under stress. While controlling the stress is your first defense, you can use smart supplementation to combat the dire effects it has on your body.

> *Magnesium:* Provides necessary energy for your adrenals—and every cell in your body—to function properly. It is closely tied to the stress response.
>
> *B Vitamins:* Play a role in balancing neurotransmitters in the brain so that you can cope with stress better.
>
> *Vitamin C:* The highest concentration of vitamin C in the body is stored in the adrenal glands. During a stressful situation, your vitamin C is rapidly used up in the production of cortisol and related stress-response hormones, so it is wise to replace these stores.

linkedin @linkedin

#digestivesupport

LinkedIn messages capitalize on your connections, allowing for better relationships to be made. #digestivesupport

Once you have connections, are you capitalizing on the LinkedIn relationship? One way to make sure that you are using your connections wisely is through LinkedIn Messages. For some peculiar reason, many people seem to forget that LinkedIn is a professional business network and that the users of LinkedIn are in fact people. You should be polite and friendly, and interact with LinkedIn members as you would with your friends or someone you met face-to-face at an event. Don't know what to say to get the conversation going? Start by congratulating people in your network when they do something praiseworthy, such as accepting a new job or honor.

In our land of abundance, it is hard to imagine that our body's cells could be starving, especially when we consume high-quality food in sufficient quantities. Yet many of our habits of affluence prohibit us from properly digesting our food, leaving our cells weak from undernourishment. Poor digestion of our consumed macronutrients (protein, fat, and carbohydrates) means poor absorption of our basic energy sources, leaving our cells hungry for energy.

Support digestion through supplementation so you are actually using the nutrients you consume. In the meantime, work on improving your digestion and health as a whole with a whole foods diet. Also identify any food sensitivities that could be wreaking havoc on your digestive tract. Remember, you may be what you eat, but you are really what you digest.

Digestive enzymes: Digestive enzymes are secreted by the pancreas and break down foods, allowing their nutrients to be absorbed into the bloodstream and used in body functions. Signs of low enzyme production include gas, bloating, low energy, and allergy-like reactions to food. Plant-based digestive enzymes in the forms of protease, amylase, and lipase can be supplemented in the short term.

Betaine hydrochloric acid: This is used to supplement the hydrochloric acid produced in your stomach. How do you know if you are low in stomach acid? Common signs include belching or gas within one hour of a meal; bad breath; brittle fingernails; and bloating or fullness shortly after eating. Supplement with hydrochloric acid while addressing the underlying reasons for low stomach acid, such as B vitamin deficiency, food sensitivities, *Helicobacter pylori* infection, excess carbohydrate or soda consumption, or hypothyroidism.

Probiotics: Probiotics are the good bacteria found in our intestines. They are needed for proper gut balance and proper nutrient assimilation. If you have just undergone antibiotic therapy or are experiencing any digestive issues, your gut bacteria might be out of whack and could benefit from probiotics.

linkedin @linkedin

#vitaminD

Find the connection that helps you just out of the blue. #vitaminD

Don't you just love when a random connection responds positively to a request you put out on your LinkedIn status? That's an example of how you just never know when connections are going to pay off. It's like they just came out of the blue! It is difficult to find this kind of connection, so you have to let it find you!

....

Did you know vitamin D is actually not a vitamin? It is closer to a hormone that affects binding sites of the human genome. And we get it out of the blue…sky! Twenty to 30 minutes of sun exposure a day during summer months is ideal to produce adequate Vitamin D in your body, but supplementation is necessary in the winter months, since food sources do not provide enough to meet daily needs. I generally recommend 5000IU of Vitamin D3 daily along with Vitamin K1 and K2 for proper utilization. Vitamin D deficiency may be a factor in the pathology of many major diseases including cancer, heart disease, and depression. Test your 25(OH) vitamin D level yearly, either at your doctor's or with a home test kit from ZRT Laboratories. Aim for levels between 50-70 ng/ml of 25(OH)D.

linkedin @linkedin

#healthyaging

Growth of your profile views is an indicator of a strong profile and network. #healthyaging

You can determine the number of times your LinkedIn profile has appeared in a search via the "Who's viewed my profile" section. What is your number of LinkedIn profile views lately? A low or declining value suggests that your LinkedIn profile is lacking the keywords that make you more search friendly. It could also mean your profile, in general, is not giving people enough reason to seek you out. Your profile headline is what people see when they scroll through users before clicking on a profile; perhaps it's a little weak.

In addition, your connections may not be high quality if they are not leading to more connections. Evaluate where you can improve the quality of your connections so your second- and third-degree connections will be more likely to have interest in you. The power of your profile and your high-quality connections can make the difference between getting found and getting ignored.

Your goal with supplementation is to support the body as it ages. Healthy aging is defined by the CDC Healthy Aging Research Network as "the development and maintenance of optimal physical, mental, and social well-being and function in older adults."

Like a strong profile and high-quality connections, your strong diet and high-quality supplements can be the difference between healthy aging and unhealthy aging.

Signs of Healthy Aging

- Outgoing personality, no signs of stress
- Feeling youthful and younger than actual age

- Normal sleep pattern with no snoring or snooze buttons
- Waist measurement of less than 35 inches for women and 40 for men
- Normal vitamin D levels (50 to 70 ng/dL)
- Low pulse (in 60 to 100 bpm range)
- Eating within needs, and on a regular schedule
- Frequent physical activity with no signs of pain
- Joint health and flexibility
- Proper digestion and regular bowel movements
- Mental and emotional health
- Healthy skin, hair, and nails
- Normal vision

Signs of unhealthy aging include: painful conditions and stiffness, memory loss, digestive problem, unintended weight loss, decreased sex drive, poor skin and muscle tone, frailty and decreased bone density. The root causes of these can almost always be traced back to poor diet and nutritional deficiencies, genetics, environmental toxins, stress and isolation, elevated blood sugar levels, lack of exercise, hormonal imbalance, and poor digestion.

linkedin @linkedin

#tweakprotocols

Keep your profile, connections, and status updated frequently. #tweakprotocols

Whether you are posting status updates, keeping your profile current at all times, writing and seeking LinkedIn recommendations, sending congratulatory messages, or posting questions and answers in LinkedIn groups, you must take action to stay visible within your network.

With each update, your network is notified. Use this to your advantage. It lets people know that you're enthusiastic and committed to creating a professional presence, and it builds the trust needed for potential relationships outside of LinkedIn.

Updating and tweaking the types and amount of supplements you take is recommended. There are many reasons for your supplement needs to change. For example, if you were taking a supplement to deal with an acute condition and the symptoms have discontinued, it is no longer needed. Or if you were supplementing while trying to improve your diet, then it may make sense to discontinue the supplement if you can reliably get that nutrient from a real food source. You may be trying to identify a sensitivity, and stopping supplements can help pinpoint if an ingredient is causing issues. Finally, you may have seasonal needs for supplementing. The best example here is vitamin D: supplementing in the summer may not be necessary, while in the winter it is. Tweaking protocols will allow you to continually get better and address your constantly changing needs.

linkedin @linkedin

#dowhatworks

Pay attention to the direct effects LinkedIn has on your professional life. Is it working for you? #dowhatworks

Tracking your number of personal connections is an obvious metric, but look at the number of discussion threads you participate in each week, as well as the number of responses your posted comments generate. Are you engaging with your target audience? Ultimately, you want people to find you on LinkedIn and then feel the need to connect with you there for further opportunities.

In the end, you must decide if your LinkedIn strategy is producing the results you are looking for. Did you find a job? Did you close that big deal? Did you create a new revenue stream? Did you network within your field? Pay attention to the direct results you gain from LinkedIn and do what works for you.

Always listen to your body. There is no one-size-fits-all supplement plan, just as there is no one-size-fits-all diet plan. If you experience negative reactions to a supplement, discontinue the supplement. If you do not feel like it is making improvements after consistent use (usually for four to six weeks), then perhaps you need a higher-quality supplement or need to adjust the dosage.

Consulting with a healthcare professional trained in functional or integrative nutrition (like me!) is extremely beneficial when figuring out what works for you.

#summary #linkedin

Set up a solid profile and add high-quality connections to gain new opportunities and achieve career advancement. #summary #linkedin

#summary #supplementwisely

Set up a solid foundational diet and add high-quality supplements to gain new levels of wellness and achieve healthy aging. #summary #supplementwisely

YOU ARE WHAT YOU RETWEET

#youarewhatyoueat

You are what you retweet. #youarewhatyoueat

You are in full control of your social media presence. You decide how much and what type of actions you will take on one or many of these platforms. In the same way, you are in full control of your diet. You decide how much and what type of food you will consume. No one is force-feeding you french fries!

Above all, stay real. With social media, keeping an authentic and genuine image online no doubt reflects your image offline. Don't forget this. This approach will benefit you in social media and, you know, life! When it comes to food, again, stay real. Fake food products in the form of manipulated and processed ingredients will never replace the food that nature has given us. A real whole foods, low-processed approach will benefit your health, and you guessed it, your life!

Refusing to take responsibility for your actions on social media is one big mistake. Thinking that anything you do or say will have no immediate or future effects on your life or the lives of others is just plain wrong. You can't hide behind your Twitter handle and expect to get away with bad behavior forever. It will always catch up with you. So if you don't take responsibility for your health now, then who will? You can't expect a poor diet to result in a great state of health. You will pay for it, whether in the form of weight gain, lost sleep, low energy, or some other health-related inconvenience. Prevention is your best solution.

It is extremely unlikely that the infiltration of social media into your life is going to slow down anytime soon. In the same way, neither will the importance of nutrition. Both social media and nutrition have the potential to make your human experience either better or worse. The best part? The choice is always yours. You are what you retweet. So retweet right.

APPENDIX

SMART CARBS

Vegetables

Artichokes
Arugula
Asparagus
Bamboo shoots
Bean sprouts
Beets
Beet greens
Bell peppers (red, yellow, green)
Broad beans
Broccoli
Brussels sprouts
Cabbage
Carrots
Cassava
Cauliflower
Celery
Chives
Cilantro
Collard greens
Cucumber
Dandelion greens
Eggplant
Endive
Fennel
Garlic
Ginger (fresh)
Green beans or snap beans
Jalapeño peppers
Jicama
Kale
Kohlrabi
Leeks
Lettuce
Mushrooms
Mustard greens
Okra
Onions
Parsley
Radicchio
Radishes
Shallots
Snow peas
Spaghetti squash
Spinach
Sugar snap peas
Summer squash (yellow, zucchini)
Sweet potato or yam
Swiss chard
Tomatoes
Turnip greens
Turnips
Watercress
Winter squash (acorn, butternut, pumpkin)

Legumes

Black beans
Chickpeas
French beans (flageolets)
Great Northern beans
Kidney beans
Lentils
Lima beans
Navy beans
Pinto beans
Split peas
White beans
Yellow beans

Grains

Brown rice
Buckwheat groats (kasha)
Bulgur (tabouli)
Corn grits
Gluten- free oats
Quinoa (a grain-like seed)
White rice
Wild rice

Other Carbs

Air-popped popcorn
Brown rice pasta
Coconut water
Corn tortillas
Kombucha
Naturally fermented sauerkraut
Organic green drinks
Organic maple syrup
Raw honey
Rice noodles

Fruit

Apples
Apricots (fresh)
Avocados
Bananas
Blackberries
Blueberries
Boysenberries
Cherries
Elderberries
Gooseberries
Grapefruit
Grapes
Kiwi fruit
Lemons
Limes
Loganberries
Mangos
Melons
Nectarines
Oranges
Papayas
Peaches
Pears
Pineapple
Plums
Pomegranates
Prunes (dried plums)
Raspberries
Strawberries
Tangerines
Watermelon

Sweeteners/Sugar Substitutes

Maltitol
Stevia (powder or liquid)
Xylitol

CRAP CARBS

Agave nectar
Bagels
Barley
Biscuits
Bran
Bread
Bread stuffing
Candy
Canned fruit in syrup
Canned vegetables
Cookies
Couscous
Crackers
Dried fruit with added sugar
Enriched flour
Flour tortillas
Fruit drinks
Fruit juice
Fruit leather
Hamburger or hotdog buns
High fructose corn syrup
Instant oatmeal
Low-fat or fat-free foods
Matzo crackers
Muffins
Orzo
Pita bread
Refined grains
Refined sugar (white, brown)
Regular honey
Rice cakes
Soda
Waffles and pancakes
White or wheat bread
White or wheat pasta

PURE PROTEINS

Bacon, additive-free
Beef and veal (grass-fed)
Bison
Chicken, duck, turkey (organic, cage-free)
Deli meats (nitrite-free, organic, uncured)
Egg white or rice protein powder
Eggs (whole, organic, free-range)
Fish (wild-caught)
Lamb
Pork (not from factory farms)
Shellfish
Undenatured whey protein powder
Wild game (venison, elk)
Yogurt (organic, full fat)

POLLUTED PROTEINS

Albacore tuna
Battery (caged) chicken, turkey
Canned light tuna
Conventional milk
Conventionally raised meats
Cool Whip
Cured meats containing nitrates
King mackerel
Most farm-raised fish, especially salmon
Processed cheese
Protein powders with artificial sweeteners
Shark
Soy milk or ice cream
Soy protein isolate
Swordfish
Tilefish
Tofu
Ultrapasteurized dairy products
Unfermented soy foods

👍 HEALTHY FATS

Avocados
Brazil nuts
Coconut milk
Cod liver oil (ideally fermented)
Extra virgin olive oil (unheated)
Extra virgin unrefined coconut oil
Fresh coconut
Ghee (clarified butter)
Grapeseed oil
Ground flaxseeds
Macadamia nuts
Nut butters
Oily cold-water fish
Olives
Organic full-fat dairy (sour cream, cream, cream cheese)
Palm oil
Peanut oil
Safflower mayonnaise
Sardines
Sesame oil
Sprouted nuts (almonds, cashews, walnuts, pecans)
Sprouted seeds (pumpkin, sunflower, sesame)
Unrefined flaxseed oil
Unrefined sesame oil

DAMAGING FATS

Canola oil
Commercial salad dressings
Corn oil
Cottonseed oil
Hydrogenated oils
Margarine
Refined oils
Regular peanut butter (with trans fat)
Soybean (vegetable) oil
Sunflower oil
Trans fats
Vegetable shortening

SNACKS

Apple and almond butter or other nut butter
Beef jerky or turkey jerky (organic)
Carrots and celery dipped in peanut or almond butter
Coconut milk smoothie with frozen fruit
Fresh fruits and vegetables
Full-fat cottage cheese with fruit
Guacamole and salsa with organic corn chips
Hard-boiled egg with unrefined sea salt
Lettuce wraps with nitrate-free deli meats and sliced avocado
Olives stuffed with tomatoes or roasted garlic
Organic whey protein shake or smoothie
Organic whole-milk yogurt and kefir
Sardines packed in olive oil or water
Sprouted raw nuts and seeds
Vegetables with hummus

👍 HAPPY FOODS

Dark chocolate, 75% or more cacao
Fresh herbs
Garlic
Hummus
Organic spices
Raw apple cider vinegar or rice vinegar
Salsa
Tamari, naturally fermented soy sauce
Unrefined sea salt

PHYSICAL SIGNS OF NUTRIENT DEFICIENCIES

The following details a simplified look at the physical signs of a variety of nutrient deficiencies. Deficiency in the nutrients mentioned is not *always* the reason for the sign, but it should be the first possible cause investigated.

Physical Sign	Possible Deficiency/Cause
HAIR	
Dry hair	Essential fatty acids (EFA)
Premature graying	Pantothenic acid (B_5)
Hair loss	Folate, B_5, B_6, B complex, EFA, Thyroid, iron stores, biotin, zinc; vitamin A toxicity
Dandruff	EFA, antioxidants (selenium especially), B_6, B complex; may also indicate low stomach acid
FACE	
Acne	Zinc, EFA, vitamin A; decreased stomach acid, overconsumption of "damaging fats"
Excess ear wax	Low essential fatty acids (EFA)
Tooth decay	B_6, minerals (especially silica, calcium, boron)
Pale tongue	Low iron levels
Dark circles under eyes	Low levels of quercetin, vitamin C; probable allergies
Dry eyes	Vitamin A
Blocked nose when drinking red wine	Molybdenum
NAILS	
Flat angle/spooning nails	Iron
Cuticle inflammation	Zinc
Ridging nails	Decreased minerals, possibly from decreased stomach acid
Hangnails	Zinc
White spots on nails	Mineral deficiency but often low zinc

SKIN	
Dry skin	EFA, vitamin A, vitamin E
Small red bumps on back of arms	Vitamin A, vitamin E, zinc, EFA; malabsorption of nutrients
Easy bruising	Vitamin K, vitamin C, vitamin E, bioflavonoids
Poor healing	Zinc
Cold hands	Magnesium; hypothyroidism, chronic fatigue
MUSCLES	
Tender calf muscles	Magnesium
Brisk knee reflexes	Magnesium
Muscle cramps	Magnesium
Shaking hands	Magnesium, vitamin B_1
OTHER	
Can't remember dreams	Vitamin B_6
Sugar craving, blood sugar swings, low blood sugar	Chromium; carbohydrate intolerance
Premenstrual syndrome	Magnesium, zinc, EFA
Mental symptoms	Any B vitamin; allergies, toxic stress
Frequent colds	Zinc, vitamin C
Poor sense of smell and taste	Zinc
Any cancer or family history of cancer	Selenium

ADDITIONAL RESOURCES

Hungry for more?

Subscribe to Jenny's monthly e-mail updates on all things nutrition and social media, by signing up on www.jennywesterkamp.com.

Free Goods!

To get a free downloadable shopping list, a guide on detoxification, and tips for fat loss, please e-mail **jenny@jennywesterkamp.com**!

Let's Chat…

Jenny is currently staring at her phone, eating a bowl of beets, sipping a green drink, thinking about something to tweet, and waiting for you to contact her.

Email: jenny@jennywesterkamp.com
Twitter: @JennyWesterkamp

P.S. Tweets are a little more exciting than e-mails, but either one works.

ABOUT THE AUTHOR

Jenny Westerkamp is a registered dietitian and the Senior Sports Nutritionist for SportFuel, Inc. in Chicago, Illinois. SportFuel is an integrative nutrition practice specializing in sports nutrition, weight loss, wellness, hair mineral analysis, and saliva hormone testing. Jenny consults one-on-one with athletes and active people, is the Team Nutritionist for the Rockford IceHogs, and assists with nutrition services for the Chicago Blackhawks organization. She is currently the President of Chicago Food and Nutrition Network and a member of Weston A. Price Foundation and American Nutrition Association.

As a senior in college, Jenny founded All Access Internships, a website dedicated to meeting the needs of the dietetics student community. Jenny graduated with high honors from the University of Illinois, Urbana-Champaign where she earned a Bachelor's degree in Food Science and Human Nutrition. She completed her dietetics training at Massachusetts General Hospital in Boston, Massachusetts.

Jenny enjoys practicing yoga, tweeting fun nutrition facts, hating on gluten, and eating organic eggs and bacon. She is the eldest in her family with five younger brothers.

E-mail or tweet Jenny with a question, comment, nutrition-related joke, non-nutrition-related joke, or any combination of these at jenny@jennywesterkamp.com or @JennyWesterkamp.

Need Supps?

Check out Jenny's online store for high quality dietary supplements providing support, as mentioned in this book, for:

- *optimal* wellness
- *increased* fat loss
- *improved* digestion
- *better* energy
- *stronger* immunity
- *superior* detoxification

There are also tasty green drinks, shakes, and bars designed to give you the most nutrition in the most convenient form!

If you don't know what supps you need, you can e-mail Jenny with your nutrition "problemos" and she'll share her best suggestions. You will just have to answer a few questions on your goals, as well as your past and current health status. Easy peasy.

Made in United States
Cleveland, OH
04 November 2026

47649176R00142